YOSEF'S STORY

Other books by Trudy J. Morgan-Cole:

Connecting
Courage to Stand
Daughters of Grace
Deborah and Barak
Esther: A Story of Courage

To order, call
1-800-765-6955.

Visit us at **www.AutumnHousePublishing.com**
for information on other Autumn House® products.

THAT FIRST Christmas

YOSEF'S STORY

TRUDY J. MORGAN-COLE

Autumn
House® Publishing
www.autumnhousepublishing.com
A Division of REVIEW AND HERALD® PUBLISHING
Since 1861

Copyright © 2009 by Review and Herald® Publishing Association

Published by Autumn House® Publishing, a division of Review and Herald® Publishing, Hagerstown, MD 21741-1119

Autumn House® titles may be purchased in bulk for educational, business, fund-raising, or sales promotional use. For information, please e-mail SpecialMarkets@reviewandherald.com

Autumn House® Publishing publishes biblically based materials for spiritual, physical, and mental growth and Christian discipleship.

Some of the details and dialogue in this book expand on the biblical story but are based on what is currently known about the times and the culture of the biblical world.

All texts are from the Holy Bible, New International Version. Copyright © 1973, 1978, 1984, International Bible Society. Used by permission of Zondervan Bible Publishers.

This book was
Edited by Penny Estes Wheeler
Designed by Ron Pride
Cover illustration by Raoul Vitale/Copyright © 2009 by Review and Herald® Publishing Association
Typeset: Bembo 12/18

PRINTED IN U.S.A.

13 12 11 10 09   5 4 3 2 1

Library of Congress Cataloging-in-Publication Data

Morgan-Cole, Trudy, 1965-
  That first Christmas-- : Yosef / Trudy J. Morgan-Cole.
     p. cm. -- (Christmas treasury series)
  1. Joseph, Saint. I. Title.
  BS2458.M67 2009
  232.9'32--dc22
                            2009012478

ISBN 978-0-8127-0499-0

DEDICATION

for Jason

CONTENTS

A Song for Mary and Joseph 8

Miryam Had a Visit From an Angel 9

Chapter One: Yosef 10

Chapter Two: Miryam 16

Chapter Three: Avigail 20

Chapter Four: The Dilemma 26

Chapter Five: The Meeting 36

Chapter Six: The Betrothal...42

Chapter Seven: The Angel's Visit 48

Chapter Eight: The Dream Ends 56

Chapter Nine: Message in the Night 64

Chapter Ten: The Letter 72

Chapter Eleven: The Wedding 80

Chapter Twelve: The Census 86

Chapter Thirteen: Israel's Deliverer 96

Chapter Fourteen: In the Hands of the Lord 102

Chapter Fifteen: Trying to Trust 108

Chapter Sixteen: No Room at the Inn 112

Messiah for the Twenty-first Century 128

A Song for Mary and Joseph

GOD said to the incredulous 4 B C Hebrews, I AM He Who walked with your fathers
    Through the Red Sea, with Moses on the Mountain,
With Abraham and Isaac to Mt. Moriah. . . .
    When they read in the Word that I would act,
Did they build a construct in their minds of My meaning? Saying of ME,
According to OUR tradition, This is what He will do, and that is how He will do it!
Did their very fingers rest on Scripture that their unseeing eyes passed over for tradition?
Yet, when I, JEHOVAH, sent forth MY Word, and acted,
    Did you hear your fathers say what you say in disbelief, This cannot be of God!
    Too bizarre! Too common! Too much against the natural order!
Ah! MY surprise moves raise suspicions which grow lushly in such climates,
    So, Faith struggles to survive, Certainty in the humble heart shimmers thinly
For a moment when whispers of delusion meet joyful recitals of visions from God.

Nonetheless, Faith will survive in shepherds' ears that heard the angels' song.
In humble hearts, Certainty will regain its shimmer
From Gabriel's blinding light of God's Messiah come to Earth.

I will ACT, and something of My ACT will stun you,
Utterly surpass and shatter reckless auguries of your messiah.

—Rhoda Wills

MIRYAM HAD A VISIT
FROM AN ANGEL . . .

For those of us who know the Christmas story it hardly seems unusual—of course an angel foretold the birth of the Messiah. But the angel's shocking message rocked Miryam's family to its foundation. No one believed it, of course. Not her parents, not her betrothed, and surely not the women who whispered behind their hands at the village well.

What could not be denied was that Miryam was unmarried and pregnant. Only the three closest to her knew that she claimed the baby was the Son of God.

Yosef is the first in a series of books written from the viewpoints of the people who lived the events surrounding Christ's birth. In this one we meet the solid, hardworking man who was blindsided by the impossible. The next books in this series will take us into the lives of Miryam, Elisheva, Zacharias, the Magi, and others.

Come along with me. Let's go through the doorway opened by author Trudy Morgan-Cole and join Yosef as he smoothes the surface of a log he's shaping into a thing of practical beauty. The sun is hot. His muscles are tired. But with his oldest son at his side and the other children playing in the work yard, Yosef is content.

—Penny Estes Wheeler

YOSEF

Yosef pulled the adze along the length of the timber, his muscles straining with the effort. Curls of wood peeled away from the rough log, revealing the smooth sheen beneath. Sweat stood out on his brow, upper arms, and bare chest, for he worked with only his loins girded in the heat of the day.

In the yard around him, his four children made themselves useful in their various ways.

Yakov, at 10, was actually old enough to be helpful, though his small hands couldn't yet master all of his father's tools. He was piling the cut ends of wood in a neat stack now, while Yehudah picked up wood chips and shavings from the ground. At 8, Yehudah wanted very much to do everything his older brother did.

The little girls sat in the shade, 5-year-old Shirah trying to keep baby Leah amused with a clapping game. Every so often Leah would wail and one of the boys would go over to help, since Shirah really wasn't big enough to pick up and soothe a lively little girl of almost 2. Most of the time, though, the girls were together, Shirah growing up much more quickly than most girls her age as she took on the responsibility of caring for her younger sister.

"It works, it works," he muttered under his breath as he kept one eye on his tools and the other on the children busy around him. He laid aside the adze and took up the plane, smoothing out the surface of the wood.

Not that there was anyone in the yard to suggest his domestic arrangements *weren't* working. It was more a matter of practicing a defense, as a skilled swordsman might practice his thrusts and parries even when no opponent was present. Yosef knew that peaceful though the afternoon seemed, his sister Rahel lived only two houses away and might appear at any minute.

And here she was, as predictable as the spring and fall rains, bustling into the yard. "Yosef! Out working in the heat of the day? You'll kill yourself. Look out, Yakov! You're going to get one of those pieces of wood in an eye! Yehudah, put that down. That's sharp!" And then, as the baby responded to the sudden increase of tension in the yard by starting to cry, she bustled over to the shaded corner by the house where the girls sat. "Leah! My poor baby. Here, let Aunt Rahel take you . . . poor little thing. No, Shirah, it's all right . . . I'll take her. Poor little thing needs a mama, don't you, sweetheart?"

"Rahel, as always, you manage to bring chaos out of order in less time than it takes a pot to boil," Yosef said as his sister drew near cuddling baby Leah in her arms.

Rahel waved away his insult as if brushing a fly from her veil. She and Yosef were the only two surviving children of their parents, and Rahel was three years his elder, so she'd had a lifetime of experience bossing him around. When he was first married, Rahel's protectiveness of her little brother had made his wife Leah's life a challenge, until Yosef had

He would keep the home he'd built for his Leah as a young bride, the home where his children had been born, and he'd raise those children there as best he could.

quietly put his foot down with Rahel and insisted she mind her own business. A few words with Rahel's husband hadn't hurt either. For the rest of his married life he had enjoyed a cordial relationship with his sister, although he could see she was constantly bursting with things she wanted to say but kept back.

But now that he was a widower—ah, Rahel had come into her own. Of course she had loved Leah—everyone did—and had been sad at her untimely death giving birth to the baby who now bore her name. But at the same time, Leah's death had given Rahel the opportunity to move into her brother's life with the kind of loving, pushy, opinionated advice and help that was her specialty. She brought meals to them, or invited Yosef's family to her house to eat. She wove and sewed and mended his children's clothes. She chided him for working too long and hard. She frequently took the three younger children to spend the day with her own brood of five.

On one count, though, Yosef had refused to give in. She wanted the children to live with her permanently—at least, until Yosef remarried, which he seemed in no hurry to do. In fact, she would have been happy to have Yosef himself move into her husband Avram's large house. But this Yosef would not agree to. He would keep up his own home, the home he'd built for his Leah as a young bride, the home where his children had been born, and he'd raise those children there as best he could. With Rahel's help, advice, and supervision, of course. And though she reveled in her role as his caretaker and right hand, she constantly nagged at him to find a new wife.

Now she was at it again. "Look at them, out here all day in the work yard. Maybe for the boys it's all right, they need to learn their trade, but the girls? Yosef, it makes no sense. What kind of life is it for them, playing in the dirt all day? Who is teaching Shirah what a young girl should know? Who is caring for Leah as only a mother could?"

"You are," he said. "You're here twice, three times a day—it's not as if any of us lacks a woman's touch." He smiled to soften the hard edge of his words. Rahel drove him mad, but he did love her.

"Yes, but how much can I do when you live up here and I live down there? I'm not a young woman any longer, you know, to come running up this hill, and I have my own children to care for. Shirah loves to play with her cousin Rivka, you know—how nice it would be if I had both of them in my house. They could make bread together, tend the fire, learn to weave and spin . . ."

"You may have my girls at your house anytime to weave, spin, or do as you please with them, Rahel," Yosef said with a sigh, "as you well know. What you cannot have is to be their mother. They have a home, and it is here with me."

"Ah, but what is a home without a mother?" she moaned. "Yosef, I know you loved

Leah. You were lucky, your marriage was a love match. And you've mourned for her long past the year of mourning. All that I understand. But you are not a love struck boy—you're a father of four children. You have a responsibility, to them if not yourself."

Yosef laid aside the plane—it was pointless trying to work while Rahel nattered at him. Shirah, freed from her child-minding responsibilities, began to chase Yehudah around the yard, while only serious little Yakov stuck to his work. "I know you're right, Rahel. I will remarry. When the time is right, and I find the right woman."

"You can't wait forever. I'll never be happy till I see you and these children settled with a new wife and mother."

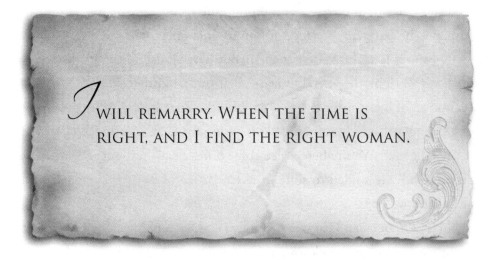

I WILL REMARRY. WHEN THE TIME IS RIGHT, AND I FIND THE RIGHT WOMAN.

He laughed and took little Leah from her arms. "You'll never be happy even *when* you see me settled, Rahel—you'll be forever finding fault with my new wife, comparing her ways to Leah's even though you weren't satisfied with Leah either. You're not pleased unless you have something to complain about, so why not leave well enough alone?"

"Because it's *not* well enough, and you know it." Her brown eyes in her round face softened and she, too, smiled. "I have been talking to Hannah, the wife of Eli. You know their young Miryam is of an age to be betrothed."

"Nonsense, Rahel." It wasn't the first time she'd brought up Miryam, daughter of

Eli, as a possible bride. "The girl is—what, 15? Scarcely older than Yakov. How could she be a mother to these four? I can't marry an untried girl."

"That's what most men want, a fresh young girl who'll bear more sons," Rahel said. "She's pretty, she's virtuous—Hannah even says she's clever. She'd be a wonderful wife."

Yosef shook his head, gave his baby daughter a kiss, and handed her back to the eager arms of her aunt. "When I marry again, I'll look for an older woman, one with some experience running a household."

Rahel pursed her lips. "You mean Avigail, of course. Well, if that's who you want, then you should speak to her."

"Don't be a fool, woman. Her husband was laid in his grave only three months ago." Avigail, widow of a metal worker from the neighboring village of Yafa, was in her mid-20s—a few years younger than Yosef himself—who had been left with three young children when her husband was killed in an accident. Yosef didn't know her well, but from the little he'd seen of her when her husband was alive she seemed kind and competent, a good wife and mother. He was in no hurry, but he thought that when her time of mourning was finished he would make an offer for her hand.

"I don't know why you want to add three more children to the ones you already have. And would Avigail want to move here, and sell her husband's business? Surely she's more likely to marry a man who will take over the business so she can stay in her own home," Rahel said thoughtfully. "I'm sure you're right—she knows her business as a wife and mother—but when all's said and done you'd be much better off with a nice young girl from right here in Nazareth. You should speak to Eli before someone else makes an offer for Miryam."

Yosef began working with the plane again, feeling the wood become smooth and shiny under his hand, thinking how simple the pleasures of work were compared with the difficulties of dealing with women. "Rahel, I have to finish this job. Take the girls home with you for the afternoon—Yehudah, too, if he wants to go. Yakov and I will join you for the evening meal. And whatever you do, don't start any marriage negotiations on my behalf!"

Chapter Two

MIRYAM

I was glad when they said unto me, Let us go into the house of the Lord.

Our feet shall stand within thy gates, O Jerusalem.

The sonorous sounds of men's voices lingered in the air for a few moments after the psalm had ended. Yosef, leaving the synagogue, found himself next to Eli the sandal-maker. "The Lord bless you," Eli said as the two men fell into step together.

"And you also," Yosef echoed. "Are you well, Eli?"

"As well as an old man can be," Eli said. "You are blessed to have your youth and your good health, despite the sorrows you have had. The Lord be praised."

"Indeed," Yosef said. He didn't always feel particularly blessed, but he tried to be grateful for what he did have—children, work, and, as Eli had pointed out, his health.

"So many worries for an old man," Eli went on. "Especially with children—well, you know about that, though you're not old yet. But when they start growing up and you think of their futures—it's a serious thing, Yosef. You have many years before you have to think of that, but my Miryam is ready to be married now—if only I could find the man good enough for her!"

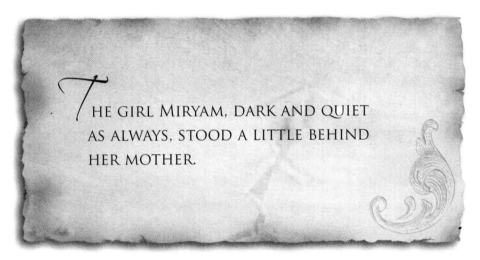

THE GIRL MIRYAM, DARK AND QUIET AS ALWAYS, STOOD A LITTLE BEHIND HER MOTHER.

Yosef hid a secret smile. Clearly Rahel had been at work, probably talking to Eli's wife Hannah and getting her to talk to Eli. "Surely no father ever thinks a man is good enough for his daughter," he said. "I'm sure I will be the same when Shirah and Leah are grown."

"No doubt, no doubt." Eli paused a moment and watched the women coming out from their section of the synagogue, taking longer than the men because they spent more time talking among themselves. Sure enough, there was Yosef's sister Rahel next to Eli's wife. The girl Miryam, dark and quiet as always, stood a little behind her mother.

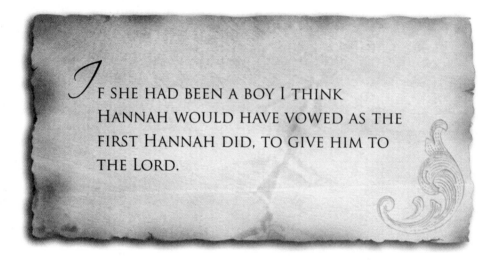

IF SHE HAD BEEN A BOY I THINK HANNAH WOULD HAVE VOWED AS THE FIRST HANNAH DID, TO GIVE HIM TO THE LORD.

"But she's a special case, my Miryam," Eli went on. "You know my Hannah, she was like Hannah the mother of Samuel in the Scriptures, barren for all the years of our marriage. How we prayed that the Lord would give us a child, like He did for Hannah and Sarah and all those women in the Scripture." Yosef had heard this story before. Nazareth was a small village, and Yosef had first heard Eli tell the joyful news of his wife's pregnancy back when it was still news, when Yosef himself was a young boy.

"Finally the Lord granted our prayer, when we had all but given up," the older man went on. "I tell you the truth, Yosef, if she had been a boy I think Hannah would have vowed as the first Hannah did, to give him to the Lord and send him to live at the Temple like Samuel. And our Miryam, though she is a girl, I have always felt she was set apart in that way, for what a good girl she is! So obedient, so faithful to the Lord, and such a quick and clever mind. You know, I've taught her the Torah, even though perhaps it's wrong to do with a girl—but she was my only one, and she so wanted to learn."

And a beauty, too, Yosef thought, eyeing the girl as she and her mother approached. Surely Eli wouldn't have any trouble finding a man willing to offer a generous bride-price for her. She wasn't the type of woman who appealed to Yosef, particularly—but that was because Leah was always and ever his standard for what a woman should be.

Leah hadn't been accounted a great beauty in her day—pretty enough, but her looks were unusual. She was tall for a woman, and had the sort of figure that made men nod with approval and say she'd bear sons—a full bosom and broad hips. Her hair was a deep reddish-brown, and her eyes and skin were paler than most Galileans. Yosef had known her since he was a boy and been in love with her since he could imagine what love was. He'd married young, obtaining his father's and Leah's father's permission when he was only 17. She was 15 then, a good age for a girl, but young men usually waited till they were a little older. He hadn't been able to bear the thought of waiting, seeing his Leah married off to another.

This girl Miryam who stood before him now with her eyes properly downcast was still a child in many ways, he pondered, no matter how clever she was or how much Torah she knew. Her hair was black, worn long and loose as befitted an unmarried maiden. She was quite short, and very slender—too thin, really, to his mind. Only the dark eyes held any allure for him, and that was perhaps because she would not look up at him. He wondered what their long dark lashes might reveal if they lifted toward him.

Chapter Three

AVIGAIL

Yosef and Yakov led their donkey, heavily laden with wood and tools, down the dusty road from Nazareth to Yafa. Yosef was glad for the company of his serious young son as the morning grew warmer and the road grew hard beneath his sandals. They had left at dawn, since the job Yosef was hired to do in Yafa would be a full day's work.

As a carpenter, Yosef worked at a variety of

jobs. He made wooden tools and furniture in his own work yard for customers who came to place an order, but there was far too little of that kind of work to support a family. He didn't like to be away from home for any length of time because of his children, so he missed out on some of the larger building projects he might have worked on in a big city such as Tiberias. However, he occasionally got a day's labor working for a wealthy patron who needed wooden doors and shutters made for a new home. One such man was Asa of Nazareth, who had liked Yosef's work enough to hire him to work on the new home his recently married son was building in Yafa.

Yosef and Yakov passed a few other travelers on the road, usually waving and calling a cheerful greeting. But when Yosef saw a cloud of dust on the road ahead he sighed. "Come, let's get off the road," he said to Yakov, leading the donkey off the rutted trail.

"Why?" Yakov wanted to know.

"The Romans are passing," Yosef said. This part of their journey took them along the broad and well-maintained Roman road which ran past Nazareth, all the way to Jerusalem in the far south. Yosef spat on the ground, as he always did when he spoke of Romans.

Now they were visible, a marching troop of uniformed men walking in perfect order, swords swinging at their sides. "Out of the way, peasant!" their leader called as he passed, even though Yosef, Yakov, and the donkey were already well out of his way.

Yakov was wide-eyed as he watched the soldiers march past. "They look splendid, Abba," he said.

"Splendid they may look, but they have no place in this land," Yosef said. He waited till they were well beyond him before leading the donkey and the boy back onto the road.

"Why do you hate the Romans so?"

"Because they rule a land that is not theirs, they force us to pay their taxes, and they declare that their emperor is lord of all the world and that all must obey and honor him. And you know, my son, there is only one Lord of this world, our God Almighty, blessed be His Name. So all who bow the knee to Caesar deny the true power of the Lord of heaven and earth."

"Oh," Yakov said. Yosef was curious about what passed through his son's mind. Yakov was so quiet, so self-contained, that he chewed most information over privately, rarely asking questions and even more rarely commenting on his thoughts. But Yosef was a private man himself, and though he often wondered what Yakov was thinking, he was not the sort to intrude on the boy's privacy with questions or unwanted information. He hoped he was doing right. Perhaps he should be making more of an effort to teach the boy, to guide his thinking. Leah would have known. While she lived, her energy and exuberance balanced Yosef's quiet caution, and he always felt the children were getting the best of both worlds between his care and Leah's. He sighed. Annoying as she was, Rahel was right. It was past time for him to find someone to share this burden with. And today, in Yafa, he intended to take a step toward righting that wrong.

He was busy all day, of course, reaching the house of his patron's son just after the morning meal and working steadily through the morning hours till noon. In the heat of the day he stopped to share the lunch he had packed with Yakov, who had been diligently helping as best he could all morning. Then, in the hour after the meal when the sun was at its zenith and working men commonly took a short rest in the shade, Yosef led Yakov to the house of Avigail, widow of Nathan the blacksmith.

The smithy was still in operation, worked by Nathan's apprentices. Yosef asked a serv–ant if he might see the mistress, and left Yakov to wait out in the courtyard with the chil–dren of the servants who played there.

The widow Avigail, who had met Yosef on a couple of previous occasions, greeted him cordially. He explained his business—a trifling matter of purchasing some nails and metal hinges, something he might easily have bought in Nazareth. He knew she would know this, and wondered if she had already guessed the real purpose of his visit.

He found himself regarding her critically as she called a servant to bring honeyed water for them to drink. She was a fine-looking woman, not striking, perhaps, but pleasant enough. She had neither Leah's glowing beauty nor the dark, mysterious charm of

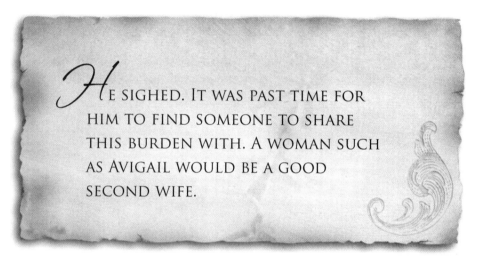

He sighed. It was past time for him to find someone to share this burden with. A woman such as Avigail would be a good second wife.

the young girl Miryam. Why was he thinking of Miryam? He had already decided that a woman such as Avigail would be a good second wife. She was wealthier than he, which might be a problem, but if she were willing to sell her husband's business and move with him to Nazareth she could manage his household for him and they would have more than enough income to support seven children.

"You must miss Nathan terribly," he said, dimly aware that this was hardly the best way to begin a proposal of marriage. Why was it so difficult? With Leah it had been the easiest thing in the world—they had exchanged words of love and secret promises, and then he had gone to talk to her father, who had been more than happy to give his daughter to the son of an old and dear friend. Why couldn't everything in life be so straightforward?

"I mean, it must be difficult for a woman alone, running a business such as this," he clarified.

Avigail inclined her head slightly in a gracious nod. "I have had to learn a great many new skills," she said. "But I have good help. My husband had two apprentices who worked with him for years, and one of those, Tobias, is skilled and experienced enough to take over management of the shop. Business is good. I hope yours is as well?"

"It is, it is." Yosef shifted the cup in his hands uneasily from one hand to the other, staring down into its depths. "And . . . and your children, they are well? Growing up now, as mine are, I suppose?"

"Yes, my son is almost of an age with your boy," Avigail said, nodding toward the courtyard where the children played together, "and my two daughters are 6 and 8 years old. They bring me much joy."

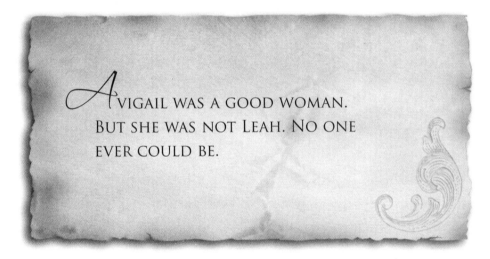

*A*VIGAIL WAS A GOOD WOMAN. BUT SHE WAS NOT LEAH. NO ONE EVER COULD BE.

"Of course . . . of course, as mine do too. But it is—ah, it is very difficult for a man, of course, without a woman's helping hand. Children need a mother." This wasn't at all how he'd planned it. He had meant to focus on *her* need, to present his proposal in a way that would make it seem he was offering her something. Instead, it now seemed he was coming to her as a supplicant, asking for a housekeeper and nurse for his children. Which, when it came down to it, was exactly what he wanted, wasn't it?

Avigail smiled again. "Children do need a mother, and a father too. I know I can never replace the good father that mine have lost, but as I am betrothed to marry again, I hope to give them a kind and caring stepfather."

"Oh, you—are you indeed? Well, what very good news. I wish you every happiness." Yosef reluctantly met her eyes and read there that she knew exactly what he'd been driving at and had offered the news of her betrothal to spare him further agony. Why had he not made sure she was still unpromised before coming here? He should have asked more questions. Rahel would have known somebody who knew. Of course he'd told Rahel nothing of this plan, more fool he.

"I have agreed to marry Tobias, my husband's apprentice, when my time of mourning is finished," she explained further. And that made perfect sense. The young man was a few years her junior, but he would no doubt be willing to accept a slightly older bride and her children in exchange for owning the business he had learned to operate.

"I wish you much joy," Yosef said, standing to go.

"And I wish you the same, Yosef bar Yakov," Avigail said gravely. "I pray the Lord will send you a kind stepmother for those children of yours."

And I pray the same, Yosef thought. He'd thought he had things worked out so well, so carefully planned, but as he walked away from Avigail's house he realized there was a touch of relief mingled with his disappointment. Yes, he was still widowed and alone; he still had all the burdens of caring for his children and fending off Rahel's well-meant advice. But he did not have to marry—yet—a woman he could never love as he had loved Leah. He didn't have to put another woman in her place in his home, in his bed, in the hearts of his children. For a while longer, he could cherish the memory of Leah and not have to think of another. Avigail of Yafa was a good woman, wise and capable and kind. But she was not Leah. No one ever could be.

He called Yakov from the courtyard and together they walked back to the house where they were working. There was still a day's work to be done and a long walk back to Nazareth at the end of it.

Chapter Four

THE DILEMMA

Some weeks had passed since Yosef's failed attempt to make an offer of marriage to Avigail. Grapes, olives, and figs were being harvested, while wheat and barley were being sown for the coming spring. The wealthier farmers, enjoying the bounty of a good crop, were inspired to expand their barns and build new ones, and there was plenty of work at this time of year for a hardworking carpenter. Yosef was up before dawn and working till after dusk most nights, sometimes spending the day working in Sepphoris or even going as far as Tiberias for a few days' work. It was impossible to keep the household running under such circumstances and after a few days of trying Yosef allowed Rahel to take the children to her home where they could be fed and watched during the day while he worked.

Yakov accompanied his father to the worksite as often as he was allowed. One day, after he had worked next to Yosef for several hours, they began the long walk home from the neighboring village where they had been helping with the construction of a rich man's house.

Dusk had already fallen by the time father and son returned home. Their house was empty, and Yosef tried to think what he might find to feed himself and the boy a quick evening meal before they fell asleep.

But no. Yakov deserved better—hot food around a friendly table. And if they ate quickly and went to sleep, Yosef would have let another day pass without seeing his younger children. He sighed, laid down his tools, and put a hand on Yakov's shoulder.

"Let's go down the hill to your aunt and uncle's house, son. They'll have something left from the evening meal for us to share, and you can sleep there with your brother and sisters and cousins."

Yakov's serious young face brightened a little, and Yosef could see how the idea of warmth and family drew him. Why would a boy want to come home to this dark and motherless house?

I should just move us all in here with Rahel and Avram, Yosef thought as they entered the bustling courtyard of his sister and brother-in-law's home. *It would be a burden to them, but if I sold my own house and my income went to benefit Avram's household, he likely wouldn't complain.* Avram was a stonemason, and their trades would match well together. Rahel would be mistress of a large, busy, blended household. And he, Yosef, would be spared the pain of trying to find another woman to take Leah's place in his heart, in his home.

From a pot over the fire Rahel scooped up fish stew into bowls for the newcomers, and each of them took flatbread with which to scoop up and eat their stew. Rahel returned to her work. The rest of the family had eaten earlier, and now the older children—her own and Yosef's— helped with the evening chores while the younger ones played on the other side of the courtyard. Avram came over to the fire and sat across from Yosef.

"The work goes well? Busy?" Avram asked.

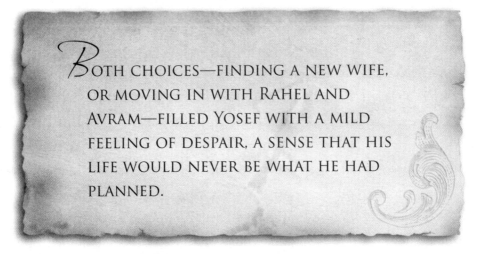

BOTH CHOICES—FINDING A NEW WIFE, OR MOVING IN WITH RAHEL AND AVRAM—FILLED YOSEF WITH A MILD FEELING OF DESPAIR, A SENSE THAT HIS LIFE WOULD NEVER BE WHAT HE HAD PLANNED.

"Busier than ever. Two other men approached me about jobs today while I worked on Eliakim's house, but I doubt I will have time to do them both. More than enough work this time of year."

"Praise the Lord," Avram said. "We must plan for seasons of famine and seasons of plenty, just as the farmers do."

"The season of plenty is also the season of hard work," Yosef said.

Avram put a hand on Yakov's shoulder. "And you, young carpenter, you are learning your father's trade," he said to the boy. "He doesn't work you too hard?"

"Oh, no, sir. I like hard work."

Avram smiled approval at the boy and met Yosef's eyes over the campfire. "He was ever that way," Yosef said. "Even as a small child, if he picked up two sticks, instead of making a game out of them or pretending to fight with swords like another boy might do, he stacked them on top of each other and went looking for more to add to his woodpile." He laughed. "Leah used to say . . ." His voice trailed off and he shook his head. He couldn't remember exactly what it was Leah used to say. He just remembered the two of them standing together in their own courtyard, in the home they had built with such love and hope for the future, smiling at their serious little boy who so wanted to do adult work. Leah had been pregnant with their second child, Yehudah, at the time.

Avram did not pursue the conversation, but turned instead to chat with the boy, allowing Yosef a moment to master his memories and his feelings. Yosef wondered what Avram thought about playing host to his brother-in-law's family. He had never formally offered to open his home to them. Of course, Rahel had suggested it half a dozen times, but the offer, if it were to come, would have to come from the husband and father. What would Yosef say, if Avram were to suddenly lean toward him across the cook fire and make that generous offer?

Yes. He ought to say yes. Then he could lay aside the dream of his own home in that little house on the hill. The dream was dead without Leah, and trying to re-create it with another woman in her place would feel like a sacrilege.

As for living out his life as an adjunct to his brother-in-law and sister, allowing his children to be raised in their home and his labor to fill their coffers instead of his own—well, it wasn't the life he'd dreamed of. But it would be the easier choice, and better for the children, no doubt. The problem was that both choices—finding a new wife, or moving in with Rahel and Avram—filled Yosef with a mild feeling of despair, a sense that his life would never be what he had planned. Neither option would make him happy. Nothing would make him happy, other than having Leah and the past back again.

The one thing that was certain was that he couldn't go on as he was doing, drifting aimlessly with no plan at all, cobbling together a life for the children in his spare time. It wasn't fair to them.

He would speak to Rahel, he decided—perhaps on the morrow. Ask if she and Avram were serious about moving Yosef's family under their roof, whether Avram would be willing to formally offer them a place in his home. It would shame Yosef to approach his sister with such a request, but it would please Rahel and it would, he was almost sure, be the right thing to do. Tomorrow.

But on the morrow he was busy again, working late, and once again took his meal late around Rahel's fire, and did not find the time to broach the subject. And the day after that was the preparation day, when all work ceased early, and the next day was the Shabbat.

He saw the girl again—Miryam, daughter of Eli—entering the women's section of the synagogue with her mother Hannah. They were very devout women. Many women, including Rahel, didn't go every Shabbat to the synagogue, considering it more properly the domain of men. But he had never seen Miryam or Hannah absent for a single Shabbat service, now that he came to think of it.

He'd decided long ago that such a young girl was unsuitable as the wife of a widower with young children, yet the thought of Miryam kept popping into his mind at unexpected times—such as during the prayers that morning at synagogue.

O Lord Almighty, Master of the Universe, You who appointed that man should not be alone but should have a helper suited to him—is it Your will that I marry again? Shall I let my sister raise my children, or should I seek a mother for them? My heart will never warm to another woman as it did to Leah, but should I be alone all the rest of my life? This girl, this Miryam, is said to be wise and virtuous. She is nothing like my Leah, yet she has her own kind of beauty. Could I come to care for her? Would she be a good wife, a good mother for Leah's children?

He bowed his head and tried to focus on the words of the service, the prayers and

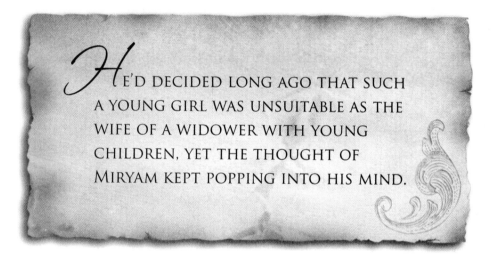

HE'D DECIDED LONG AGO THAT SUCH A YOUNG GIRL WAS UNSUITABLE AS THE WIFE OF A WIDOWER WITH YOUNG CHILDREN, YET THE THOUGHT OF MIRYAM KEPT POPPING INTO HIS MIND.

readings from Scripture, hoping all the time for a hint of the Divine will, a sign that would point him which way to go.

Don't be a fool, he chided himself as he left the synagogue with the other men. *You are no Gideon. No angel has called you to lead an army into battle. Why should you expect signs and wonders? The Lord Almighty has given you a simple decision to make: marry, or remain in your brother-in-law's house. You need no wet fleece to make that decision, only the good sense God has given you.*

Enough of this time-wasting, this endless thinking about what to do. He would do it today. He would ask Rahel to speak to Avram.

As the men gathered to talk and wait for their womenfolk on the steps of the syn-agogue, Yosef turned for his brother-in-law's home alone, not even waiting for Avram to accompany him. Rahel would be home with the children; the Shabbat meal would be ready, with most of the preparation having been done the day before. Time to go home. Time to begin thinking of it as home.

Then as he walked away he felt a hand on his shoulder. "Yosef, my carpenter friend," an elderly voice said.

He turned to see Eli the sandal-maker. His wife and daughter stood a little apart. "Good Shabbat to you, Eli."

"I wonder if you will come to my house today, and be our guest for the Shabbat meal," Eli said. "You would do us great honor."

"How very kind of you, Eli. I would be glad to join you." Yosef wondered, as he fell into step beside the older man, if this was more of Rahel's doing. She had stopped agitating him about finding a wife ever since he had allowed the children to stay at her home, and he'd assumed she was happy with the present situation, with her own role firmly in charge of her brother and nieces and nephews. But perhaps she—or more likely Avram—didn't want that burden indefinitely, and were taking steps to help Yosef along in his reluctant quest to find a wife.

Whatever the reason, he found himself stepping into the courtyard of Eli's house, where he had never before been a guest, sitting near the cooking fire as Miryam and a servant girl ladled spiced lentils onto his plate.

The girl's demeanor was perfect. She kept her eyes down. She did not look at the male visitor but served him his meal, passed a plate of bread whenever his was empty, brought oil for him to dip his bread, and lemon water for him to drink. Yosef wished he could speak to her. He was curious about her now, this girl whose virtues had been described to him so many times. If he could talk to her for himself, he might have a hint, a clue of whether she could in any way fill the empty place in his heart and home.

But this was no independent widow woman like Avigail of Yafa. This was Eli's virgin daughter, who had no business speaking to a man outside her immediate family. Any marriage arrangement made for Miryam would be made between her father and a prospective husband. The girl herself might not even meet her bridegroom until the betrothal ceremony, and certainly would not be alone with him.

One other guest sat at Eli's table that Shabbat, a widower like Yosef, but a much older man of Eli's own age. His name was Ehud, and he had been a leatherworker, but his hands were now cramped and curled with arthritis so that he could not work any-

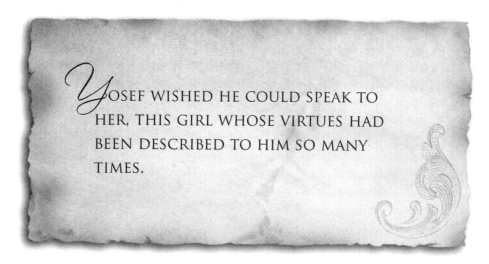

YOSEF WISHED HE COULD SPEAK TO HER, THIS GIRL WHOSE VIRTUES HAD BEEN DESCRIBED TO HIM SO MANY TIMES.

more. He resided in the home of his daughter and her husband, who had taken over his craft, and pursued his great passion, which was the study of Torah.

As the two older men fell into a discussion of the laws of Moses, Yosef excused himself politely, following Eli's gestured instructions to find the privy out behind the house. His brief journey took him past the corner of the courtyard where Eli's wife and daughter sat fanning themselves in the shade of a terebinth tree. Normally they would be busy along with their servant girl, cleaning up after a meal and preparing for the next one, but during these Shabbat hours even the endlessly busy women enjoyed a little rest. Yosef always thought Rahel looked uneasy on Shabbat, as if she didn't know how to sit still, but he could hear Hannah's and Miryam's voices in a quiet murmur of conversation, as if they welcomed the time to just sit and rest and talk.

On his way back to rejoin the men he passed the women's corner again, but now their voices were a little louder. Still out of sight, he paused for a moment, knowing he shouldn't eavesdrop but still curious about this girl. He wanted to catch her in an unguarded moment.

His curiosity was rewarded beyond his wildest dreams as he heard Hannah insist, "It's an excellent match, Miryam! If he offers, you would be a fool not to accept."

Miryam's reply was so low Yosef couldn't catch the words, though to his shame he leaned closer to the wall so that he might hear more.

"Oh, it's no easy life, I know, taking over house and children and husband from a woman who's passed away, but you could do it. You're a good housekeeper."

This time he could hear Miryam's voice, lower and quieter than her mother's. "It's not the work I fear, nor stepping into another woman's place. I just want to know that this is God's will for me, and I'm by no means sure of that."

"God's will? My darling girl, what could God's will be for you but to marry a good man and bear his children? I have known from the time you quickened in my womb that the hand of the Lord was upon you, but I don't imagine that you're to be a prophetess or judge like Devora. You will serve the Lord by being a good wife and mother."

"As you have been, Mama," the girl said, and Yosef could hear the rare smile in her voice before their words again became so soft he could not hear.

He was caught then, not wanting to walk past and have them guess that he had overheard their conversation, so he backtracked and circled around the courtyard the other way, returning at last to sit with the other men who were still talking about Torah.

"You know what the Scripture says about our father Adam?" Eli said, leaning closer to Yosef. "The Lord said, 'It is not good for man to be alone.' A man such as yourself, with a household to manage and children to raise—you cannot afford to mourn too long. How long since your wife passed away?"

"Two years, now," Yosef said shortly. It was two years and three months almost to the day. Little Leah's birthday was his wife's day of death. A heavy burden for the girl to carry; he would wait till she was older to tell her. He drew a deep breath. "It is true. My children need a mother."

"My Miryam is of marriageable age, you know," Eli said, apparently deciding Yosef would never raise the topic himself without a nudge.

"She is still very young, is she not?"

"She has just turned 16."

"My oldest boy is nearly 11," Yosef said softly. "Miryam is young to be a mother to such a brood, though she seems like a wise and virtuous girl."

"I would like to see her well matched before I die," Eli said. "You know how precious she is to me. I would hate to see her go to some man who would not value her, who might treat her poorly."

"You could trust that I would treat her well," Yosef said. "But if I were to offer for her, I would like to be sure the match was not against her will and that we would be suited to each other. Do you think I might meet her, and speak to her?"

Eli nodded, considering the request—not customary, but by no means unheard-of. He stroked his beard. "What better time than the present?" he said. "You are here, in my house. Speak with my daughter now, and perhaps we will talk of marriage later."

Chapter Five

THE MEETING

Once, as a boy about Yakov's age, Yosef had ridden in a cart that broke loose from the donkey's harness and careened wildly downhill, out of control. What he'd felt that day, he felt now as he stood in the courtyard of Eli's home waiting to be introduced to Miryam. He had come here with no intention of arranging a marriage. Now, suddenly, he was about to meet and talk with the girl, and her father confidently expected that after a brief conversation Yosef would come back to him with an offer of marriage. If he talked to her and didn't make an offer, it would seem like a slap in the face both to Miryam and her family, as if he had judged her unsuitable.

He had no idea how he'd gotten himself into this situation. Hadn't he decided, just that morning in the synagogue, that he would definitely put aside all thoughts of marriage and make his home permanently with his sister and brother-in-law?

Why, then, was he standing here as Eli led Miryam toward him? Why was he trying to think what to say to this young girl before the eager eyes of her mother, father, and an old family friend?

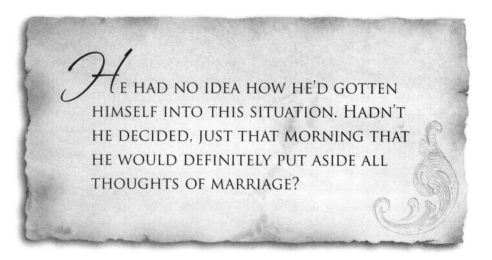

HE HAD NO IDEA HOW HE'D GOTTEN HIMSELF INTO THIS SITUATION. HADN'T HE DECIDED, JUST THAT MORNING THAT HE WOULD DEFINITELY PUT ASIDE ALL THOUGHTS OF MARRIAGE?

 osef bar Yakov, carpenter, this is my only daughter, Miryam, my gift from God," Eli said formally. Then he stepped back a bit and retreated to the bench where his wife sat a little ways away. Ehud joined Hannah and Eli there. The three older people pretended to talk amongst themselves but Yosef could see them glancing over frequently as if to gauge how his conversation with Miryam was progressing.

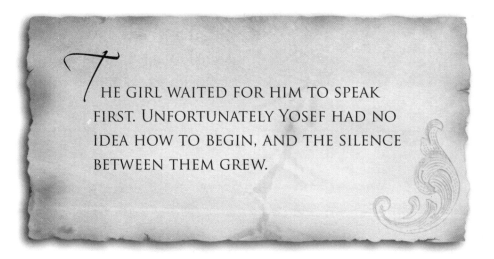

THE GIRL WAITED FOR HIM TO SPEAK FIRST. UNFORTUNATELY YOSEF HAD NO IDEA HOW TO BEGIN, AND THE SILENCE BETWEEN THEM GREW.

The girl waited, as was appropriate, for him to speak first. Unfortunately Yosef had no idea how to begin, and the silence between them grew. Finally he blurted out, "Many people have told me that you are a godly and virtuous maiden who would be a good wife." Awkward, but at least it was true.

She dropped her eyes and addressed the ground. "If it is the Lord's will, I hope to be a good wife, sir."

"Yet—I must make a confession," Yosef blundered on. "I . . . ah . . . I overheard, a few moments ago when you were talking with your mother. You seemed—unsure, whether you would accept a proposal of marriage."

Still the modest downcast eyes, the reserved demeanor so appropriate for an unmarried girl. He should have approved, but he couldn't helping thinking of Leah's frank gaze and hearty laughter. Of course, he had never been a stranger to Leah. This girl met him as a stranger, and how else should she behave?

"I only wish to be sure that what I do with my life is according to God's will for me," Miryam said. "That matters more than anything else." Her dark eyes met his for a moment, then glanced down again.

That tiny glance made him bold, as if it promised him a chance of getting to know the real woman beneath her veil.

"I, too, struggle to know the Lord's will," he admitted. "My sister tells me I have a duty to marry again and provide my children with a mother."

Now she looked full at him, her large brown eyes fringed with darker lashes. "But your heart is not inclined that way?" she asked.

"I . . . do not know."

She continued to meet his eyes, as if the maidenly shyness she had shown before was only a cloak that could be dropped at will. In the eyes that met his he saw a keen intelligence and curiosity.

"That is the great question, is it not?" she said. "How do we know God's will, when our own inclinations lead us one way and the guidance of those around us leads us another?"

"We look to the Law and the Prophets to guide us, of course," he replied.

"Then there is no question. I must marry, for to marry and have children is a woman's duty," Miryam said. She didn't sound particularly happy with this conclusion.

"Then you, too, have your doubts about marrying?" he asked. "Why?" He remembered suddenly when he was her age, in love with his childhood playmate Leah, terrified someone would offer for her hand in marriage before he himself was old enough to do so. "You are not . . . there is no one else to whom your heart belongs, is there?"

"No one but God," Miryam said, still looking steadily at him.

"Of course. But, as you say, He has already called you to your destiny as a wife and mother. The only question is—has He called you to be *my* wife, or someone else's?"

Miryam allowed herself a small smile. He was beginning to get her measure, and sensed that her quietness was not shyness or even maidenly modesty. Rather, she ex-emplified the proverb that still waters ran deep. Behind those quiet eyes was a mind as sharp as his own and a will as strong—stronger, perhaps.

"I have a second confession to make, Miryam," he said, spreading his hands like a man who shows his enemy he carries no weapon. "Did you ever know my wife, Leah?"

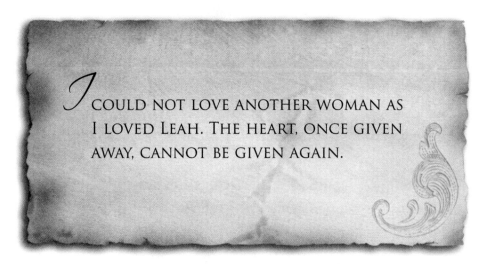

I COULD NOT LOVE ANOTHER WOMAN AS I LOVED LEAH. THE HEART, ONCE GIVEN AWAY, CANNOT BE GIVEN AGAIN.

Miryam inclined her head slightly. "I met her. She was a good woman."

"She was, and I loved her dearly. I have been reluctant to marry again because I know I could not love another woman as I loved Leah. The heart, once given away, cannot be given again. But I would treat a wife with care, gentleness, and respect. Caring for four growing children is not easy, I know, but I would do all I could to make your task easier if you would help me bear that burden."

"Thank you for telling me that," she said gravely. "Should I assume, then, that you will make an offer of marriage to my father?"

He had not expected her to ask this quite so bluntly, but he knew her well enough after even this short conversation to know that she would neither offer nor expect less than complete honesty. He took her hand, and while she did not clasp his warmly, neither did she pull away.

"I think I will, Miryam. Would that please you?"

"I hope you will not mind if I pray about it," she said. "But I know my father and mother will advise me to marry you, so unless the Lord leads me otherwise, I think that my answer will be yes."

Yosef couldn't help comparing the moment to the day he'd whispered to Leah he was going to ask his father to make an offer for her. How they'd laughed together, clasped hands and stolen a secret kiss. So different from this serious agreement with this serious young woman. He hoped he was not making a terrible mistake. His heart felt cold in his chest.

"I, too, will pray to know God's will," he said. "I hope we will talk again, Miryam."

She nodded. "If the Lord orders it, so it will be."

Chapter Six

THE BETROTHAL

The betrothal was formalized at Eli's house a few weeks later, at a dinner to which both families were invited. Yosef led his sister and her husband, all her children and all his own, into the courtyard of Eli's house. Eli waited with Miryam's hand in his, Hannah hovering in the background while several of Miryam's aunts, uncles, and cousins looked on.

Eli placed Miryam's hand in Yosef's. "This

man, Yosef the carpenter, has asked for my daughter, Miryam, in marriage. Today they are betrothed to one another. Next year at the time of the wheat harvest they will be married, and Yosef will take Miryam into his home."

Yosef studied the dark, thoughtful eyes of his bride-to-be for a moment before he, too, spoke in a voice that was intended to carry throughout the courtyard. "I vow that I will take Miryam, daughter of Eli, as my wife, and be a good husband to her. I thank my friend Eli for the privilege of bringing Miryam into our family."

Impossible not to remember, not to compare it to the day when he and Leah had first been pledged to each other so many years ago. But he brushed that thought aside as he might brush sawdust from a finished piece of work. This was today, and his bride-to-be was Miryam. Beautiful, intelligent, quiet Miryam, who had already

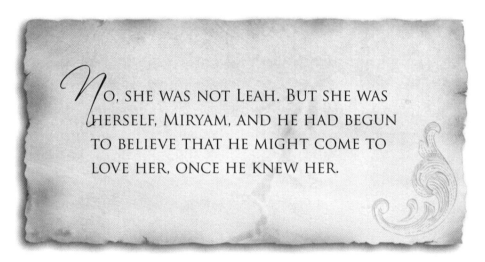

No, she was not Leah. But she was herself, Miryam, and he had begun to believe that he might come to love her, once he knew her.

begun to fascinate and intrigue him. No, she was not Leah. Nor was she the capable, experienced household manager he had imagined might make a good second wife. But she was herself, Miryam, and he had begun to believe that he might come to love her, once he knew her. She would not be an easy woman to get to know, but he liked what he had seen so far.

He watched her from across the courtyard as the men sat and ate and the women served. She seemed as quiet among the other women as she had been with him, but again he had the impression of one who was quiet because she was watchful and thoughtful, not because she was dull or empty-headed. He watched her, too, with the children, saw how she knelt down in the dust to talk to Shirah face to face, how she swept Leah up into her arms when the little girl tripped and hurt her knee.

A moment later, Miryam crossed the courtyard with Leah still in her arms. "She wants her Papa; no one will do but Papa," Miryam said. "Her Aunt Rahel tried to take her, but she cried and cried for you."

"She's become very used to me caring for her," Yosef said. "Rahel does so much for her, but sometimes she still clings to me." He looked down to examine the scratch on her bare plump knee.

"It's nothing serious, hardly bleeding at all," Miryam said. "I think she cried more from the surprise than the pain." Leah's sobs had turned to sniffles now as she buried her head in her father's shoulder. Miryam watched her for a moment, then said, "It will not be easy for her to adjust to having a stepmother."

"In some ways, no." He paused. "Yet I suppose that in other ways it will be easier, since she is the only one who has no memories of her mother. I think she will quickly come to love you, and I can see that Shirah and Yehudah like you and trust you already."

"They are very sweet children," Miryam said. Her eyes darted to Yakov, who was sitting quietly among the men, listening to their conversation rather than playing with the other children.

"Yes, that one will be more of a challenge," Yosef answered her unspoken thought. "His mother's death hit him hard, and he is more attached to me than even the younger ones are."

"And he's not an easy child to get to know," Miryam observed. "Obedient and dutiful, but watchful and quiet, sharing little of his thoughts." She smiled briefly, a smile that warmed her face like a shaft of sunlight appearing from behind heavy clouds, then as quickly disappeared. "He reminds me of myself."

"Then perhaps you will be exactly the stepmother he needs," Yosef said, hoping it would be true.

> WITH MIRYAM HE WAS EMBARKING UPON SOMETHING ENTIRELY NEW—NOT HIS FIRST BOYISH LOVE, BUT A NEW STAGE OF HIS LIFE WITH A NEW WOMAN. AND SOMEWHAT TO HIS OWN SURPRISE, YOSEF REALIZED HE WAS READY FOR THAT.

"Everyone is watching us," Miryam said—and, sure enough, all the gathered relatives, men and women, were darting little glances their way, smiling and whispering to each other, everyone anxious to see how the newly betrothed couple were getting along.

Miryam held out her arms. "Perhaps Leah will come back with me now?"

The little girl, her bout of crying ended and her scraped knee quite forgotten, went happily back to Miryam's arms and she took her to rejoin the women and children on the other side of the courtyard. Yosef joined the group of men again. He knew they were curious, and he decided there was no point being mysterious or evasive. "Eli, your daughter is a gem," he said to his future father-in-law. "She is so good with the children. I think it will be a very short time before they begin to look to her as a true mother."

During the following weeks, Yosef visited Eli and Hannah's home several more times, always with his children in tow, though without the many other relatives who had attended the betrothal dinner. These visits gave a chance for both him and the children to get to know Miryam better, and he liked what he learned about the grave, quiet girl who would be his wife. In a way, it was good that she was so different from his Leah. If she were similar, he might begin to imagine her as a replacement, and she would be bound to disappoint. But with Miryam, he could tell himself, he was embarking upon something entirely new—not his first boyish love, but a new stage of his life with a new woman. And somewhat to his own surprise, Yosef realized he was ready for that.

But he wasn't ready for the conversation he had with Miryam one day near the end of winter. Nothing could have prepared him for that.

Chapter Seven

THE ANGEL'S VISIT

iryam sent a messenger—her young cousin Ari—to Yosef's home, asking him to come to Eli's house, as she needed to talk with him about something important. Yosef sent the boy back with the reply that he would come that night after the evening meal. Leaving the children with Rahel, he walked across the village, wondering what could be so urgent that his betrothed would send such a message. She

was an unusual young woman, he knew that much, but her behavior since their betrothal had always been perfectly conventional and appropriate. This was out of the ordinary, and he couldn't even guess what to expect.

He knew something was wrong as soon as he entered the courtyard of Eli's home. This was a place where a sense of peace usually reigned, where Eli sat quietly working or talking to his visitors while the women went about their business in the background. Today the sound of Eli's hammer was still and he heard no clattering of pots as the women prepared the meal. Eli sat on a bench against the wall, Miryam beside him. Hannah stood a little to the side, her hands knotted in her apron.

Miryam's veil was pulled over her forehead and partly up over her mouth, but even in the small space bared Yosef could see that she was upset. Her dark eyes, when she briefly raised them to look at him, were red-rimmed as if she had been crying. Serene Miryam, so guarded and quiet, who revealed so little of her emotions. What could have happened to provoke such a response?

Eli sighed deeply.

Yosef took his seat on a stool across from Eli and Miryam. Everybody sat in silence for a moment. Yosef looked first to Eli, wondering what his future father-in-law had to say, but Eli only looked over at Miryam. And Miryam was silent. It was not her accustomed, contained silence but an agitated, edgy silence, as if she had much to say but could not find the words to begin.

Finally she spoke, her dark eyes meeting his and then shifting away again. "Yosef, there is something I have to tell you, but you must know that it is going to be difficult and you may not understand." She looked down, and her hair fell across one eye.

"You may not believe me. Mama and Papa—I'm not even sure they believe me." She glanced at her parents, as if hoping they would challenge this statement and assure her that they did, in fact, believe her. But Eli remained silent and Hannah shook her head slowly, as if in amazement.

Miryam took another deep breath. "I had . . . a vision," she began. "An angel . . . an angel of the Lord appeared to me."

"A vision? An angel?" Yosef echoed.

"Yes."

She was right—it was difficult to believe, and Yosef was a bit taken aback. Of course he believed that the Lord sent visions to devout and faithful men—yes, and women too, for he knew his Scriptures, knew of prophetesses like Devorah and Huldah. That an angel might even appear to such a person—it was not beyond possibility.

But, though Yosef would have said if asked that he firmly believed in angels and in visions, he also believed—without thinking about it too much—that such miraculous events were confined to the age of the Scriptures, to the great men and women of the past. An ordinary village girl in a town like Nazareth, a sandal-maker's daughter and soon-to-be carpenter's wife, having visions and seeing angels? If he'd heard such a thing of anyone but Miryam, Yosef would have suggested the poor girl had perhaps been out in the hot midday sun too much, that she was more likely to have a fever than a visitation from the Most High.

But, Miryam. If he were to pick a simple village girl to whom God might appear—and God's chosen messengers in the past had often been humble and common people, Yosef reminded himself—who more likely than Miryam? She was so devout, so dedicated to God, and she had that absolute certainty that she had spoken of before, that her life was touched by God. Maybe she had foreseen this all along. He looked in her eyes and, although they were troubled, he saw no hint of madness or fever, nor none of doubt or uncertainty. Whatever the vision had been, she was sure of it.

He took a risk. He was intrigued by this girl, had been since he'd met her, and though he didn't love her as he'd loved Leah, he surely trusted her. He had faith in her. And he believed that someday he would come to love her, and she him. Love could not be born in mistrust. So he took a deep breath and said, "I believe you, Miryam. If you say you had a vision of an angel from the Lord, then I believe you."

He looked for relief to flood her face, but there was none. Instead she said, "There is more. I haven't told you what the angel said."

"No? Then tell me." Her manner was forbidding, and she was clearly still nervous. A sudden thought occurred to him. Had the vision told her not to marry him? And if so, was it really the word of the Lord, or the manifestation of her own doubts and fears about the marriage? Either way, he would not be able to marry her. Yosef was surprised to realize how much this disappointed him.

"The angel told me I would bear a child. A special child—he said it would be called the Son of the Most High. I think he meant it would be the Messiah, our Deliverer."

"What?"

Yosef was relieved she wasn't turning aside from their marriage, but—a message about the child they would have someday? Such an exalted destiny? Surely this must be Miryam's own wishful dreaming. Could such a thing be?

"Miryam, I—this is—the angel really said we would have a child who would be the Lord's Anointed One?" He felt as if he were playing a game with his children, pretending to enter into the unbelievable world her words had created.

"No. You still don't understand." Her eyes held his steady but her fingers, plucking at the fabric of her robe, betrayed her agitation. "Not our child—*my* child. The child in my womb right now. The angel told me I am with child, right now."

"What? But that is—impossible."

"Exactly. Impossible. But it's true, Yosef." For the first time her voice trembled, and tears shone in the dark eyes. "I had the vision weeks ago, but I told no one until time passed, until I was sure of the signs in my own body. I am with child, Yosef. I have never been with any man. I have never been touched by a man, but I am going to have a baby."

Yosef had no idea what to say. Had she gone mad? That would be the kinder explanation. But there was no madness in Miryam's eyes. Was there guilt? For that was the more likely explanation—she had a guilty secret, another man, and had come up with this incredible story to cover it up.

He searched her face. She, who had always met his eyes so fearlessly, looked away, unable to sustain her gaze. She was guilty. She had to be.

Or perhaps—his mind floundered, hoping to find a way to exonerate her—she was hiding not guilt but shame. Had some man caught her unawares, forced her, and she was not willing to admit it and point the finger of blame? Perhaps such an attack might have unbalanced her mind, and she really believed the story of the angel and the holy child?

Yes. That must be it. For he could not imagine Miryam telling a deliberate lie.

"Miryam, this is . . . folly," he said at last. "I know it must seem real to you, but you must know that it is blasphemy to speak of such things falsely—angels, visions, the Messiah. You cannot use the Lord's name to cover a man's sin. You must tell your parents, and me, what really happened."

"But I've told you!" she protested, and now the tears really did spill out of her beautiful eyes and down over her cheeks.

He looked at Eli and Hannah, seeking their support. But to his surprise, he met a cold look from Eli. "Indeed, Yosef. My daughter's far-fetched story of angels and Messiahs should not be used to cover up a man's sin. Now, is there anything you want to tell me?"

"I . . . what? What has this to do with me?" Yosef honestly didn't understand, for a moment, what the sandal-maker was implying.

Eli lifted his head, his eyes boring into Yosef. "You are betrothed to my daughter, and she is with child. Do I need to make myself any clearer?"

"What? Eli—surely, surely you cannot think that I would dishonor you, and Miryam, so?" Yosef was shocked, but at least he understood now. And offended though

SHE, WHO HAD ALWAYS MET HIS EYES SO FEARLESSLY, LOOKED AWAY, UNABLE TO SUSTAIN HER GAZE. SHE WAS GUILTY. SHE HAD TO BE.

he was, he couldn't help seeing the sense in Eli's position. If a betrothed young girl suddenly turned out to be pregnant, why look for a stranger lurking in a dark corner when the most likely suspect was the man to whom she had already been promised?

It made sense. And it might even make sense that Miryam would make up an outrageous story to cover their guilty secret. But the truth was, as Yosef well knew, that there was no guilty secret at all. He and Miryam had never spent a moment alone together, and he certainly had never taken advantage of her. He would never do such a thing! Even when he was a young boy, hot-blooded and madly in love with Leah—no, never. True, he and Leah had had more opportunity to be alone together, growing up as friends and neighbors, and there had been a few stolen kisses and embraces before the wedding day—but even as a young man Yosef would never have taken advantage of his bride before the wedding night. How much less so now, when he was a respectable widower, and she an innocent young girl in her father's house?

He tried to put this into words for Eli—stumbling, halting words that he hoped conveyed his honest innocence and bewilderment rather than guilt. He couldn't read the older man's expression, but when Yosef finally ran out of words, protesting again that he had never laid a hand on Miryam, Eli's gaze swung back to his daughter.

"Miryam, your betrothed swears he has not taken advantage, that he has not gotten you with child. Does he speak the truth?"

"Of course he does, Father!" she said desperately. "It's as I told you—I am a virgin! I have never been with a man!" She was crying openly now, wringing her hands. Some part of Yosef wanted to gather her in his arms, soothe and protect her. But he made no move toward her. He still couldn't fully grasp what was going on.

"Then if it is not Yosef, it is some other man." Eli rose to his feet. "My daughter, you have dishonored not only yourself, your father and mother, and the Lord. You have also dishonored this good man who was going to make you his wife. How could you do such a thing?"

"No! No! I swear it's not true!"

Now someone did move to put an arm around Miryam—neither Yosef nor Eli, but her mother. Hannah sat on the bench and drew the sobbing girl to her lap, holding her tight. But when, at last, she spoke her voice was firm.

"Miryam, you must stop this. The Lord can forgive sins, but not a sin that is hidden and denied, kept in the dark. Tell the truth, confess your sin, and we will seek how it may be made right. Perhaps this other man will marry you instead . . ." her voice dropped, "if he is not already married."

"There is no other man!" Miryam howled. She, who always seemed so self-possessed and sure, now seemed like a little child, insisting that her make-believe world of dolls and fables was real. Yosef returned again to his earlier thought: her mind had been unbalanced.

"My friend, there maybe is another explanation," he said to Eli. "Perhaps the man who got Miryam with child took her by force. If she was forced, perhaps with violence, she may not be thinking clearly. It may be she really believes this story of the angel—perhaps she cannot bear to remember what truly happened."

He saw how Eli and Hannah looked relieved at once, seizing on his explanation as one that absolved their beloved daughter both of wantonness and of lying. "Is it so, my dove?" Hannah asked. "Calm down, now, and try to think. Did a man—some stranger, perhaps—take advantage of you? Force you to lie with him? It will be painful, but so much better if you can recall what really happened."

"I swear the man will be punished," Eli vowed.

But still Miryam shook her head and wiped away tears. "No, no, no! There was no man—I would remember. I would not lie about such a thing. There was a vision, and an angel, and I knew nothing more until I began to notice the signs that I was carrying a child. Then I knew the vision was real, and the angel's words were true."

Miryam's words were choked out between sobs, but there could be no doubt they were sincere. Yosef tried once more. "Miryam, calm yourself, and try to remember the truth. If you tell us what truly happened, we can help you."

In reply the girl only buried her face in her hands and cried harder. Yosef looked at her bent head, feeling completely at a loss. Had she betrayed him, or had she been the victim of a terrible crime? And whichever the case, why could she not tell the truth rather than insisting on a lie that no one could ever believe?

Chapter Eight

THE DREAM ENDS

In the days that followed, the knot of dread in the pit of Yosef's stomach grew harder and more painful. He visited Eli's home almost every day, but Miryam's story never changed. She calmed down, no longer broke down and cried, but seemed gripped in an almost icy calm. But she stuck firmly to saying that she had been visited by an angel and the child she was carrying was placed in her womb by the Holy Spirit.

"Do you not believe in miracles?" she asked Yosef three days after she had first told him the news. He had come once again, hoping to talk sense into her, though he doubted it would do much good. He found it harder and harder to cling to the belief that she was the innocent victim of an assault. Her steely determination to stick to her angel story made it seem far more likely she was hiding a guilty conscience.

And what then? Whether or not she named her partner in sin, she was unfaithful to him. Betraying one's betrothed was as serious as adultery, even though she and Yosef were not yet husband and wife. By the strictest interpretation of the law, he could demand she be stoned to death. While he would never do such a thing, nor would most men, he would certainly have to publicly repudiate her, let the village know what she had done, and lay aside any plans of marrying her. What kind of future could she have after that?

"Of course I believe in miracles, Miryam," he said patiently. He sat beside her on the bench in the courtyard. Her father and mother were both going about their accustomed duties not far away, neither one able to keep their minds on their work. Both pairs of eyes kept drifting toward Miryam and Yosef, deep in talk. "But this is no miracle. This is madness."

"What of the women of the Bible to whom the Lord gave a child? What of Hannah, or Rebeckah—or Sarah, 90 years old?"

"What of them, Miryam? Yes, the Lord opened wombs that were barren, but those women had husbands! The Lord does not give a child to a virgin! There are no such stories in our Scriptures. What you speak of sounds like the fables the Greeks tell about their gods!"

Yosef was not an educated man, but in Galilee, working as a tradesman, it was impossible not to rub shoulders with Gentiles. He had worked alongside some in Sepphoris and Tiberias, and heard their incredible stories of gods who took on human form to mate with mortal women and give birth to half-divine children.

Miryam had obviously heard such stories too. "No, no, it was nothing like that!" she insisted. She looked up to meet his eyes. Josef looked away.

"I do not know the moment when it happened," Miryam said with a little sigh, "nor did the Lord come to me as a man. Such a thing would be blasphemy! I only knew when the angel told me."

"How dare *you* speak of blasphemy, Miryam?" The anger that had been carefully kept beneath the surface now came to the fore, coloring his words. "You are treading perilously close to it with this story of a divine child. You must stop this nonsense, now, or you will be guilty of blasphemy as well as fornication. Speak the truth, and honor God."

This time there were no tears, no wild pleading or begging. She simply looked at him clearly and steadily, her large dark eyes dry and serious. "I am speaking the truth, Yosef. But I see now that I will never convince you or my parents or anyone else of that. Perhaps this is part of the burden the Lord has given me—to do this task for Him, and know that everyone will always believe me a sinner."

Yosef left Miryam's house that day certain he would never set foot there again. He would meet with her father publicly, in the village where everyone could see, and break the betrothal contract. He would tell the world that Miryam was faithless and a sinful woman, and leave her to whatever fate her father and the village elders deemed appropriate for her.

But even as Yosef formed the picture in his mind, tried to imagine himself saying the words, he knew he could not do it. Oh, the betrothal must be broken, of course. He could not marry Miryam. Whether she was deceitful, unfaithful, or perhaps even mad, there was no possibility she could be his wife. But he was still fond of her and believed, somehow, that she was a good woman despite the strange events of the last few days. And there were her parents to consider, too. They were good people and they had placed all their hopes on their only daughter. There would be enough pain and shame for them to endure without Yosef making a public spectacle of Miryam.

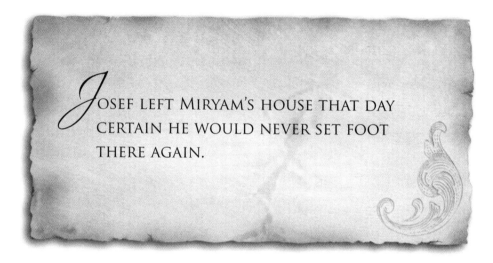

JOSEF LEFT MIRYAM'S HOUSE THAT DAY CERTAIN HE WOULD NEVER SET FOOT THERE AGAIN.

By the time he reached his sister's house, the decision was made. He would end the betrothal privately, without making any public declaration. Miryam would be the focus of enough attention and scrutiny over the next months, without his making it worse.

As he stepped over the threshold he heard the children's shouts. His heart fell a little more. The children had grown attached to Miryam—the younger ones, at least. Yakov held himself apart from her, as if he were not quite certain he should trust her, but the other three had taken to her at once. And when Yosef had brought them to visit Eli's home, they had been eager to play with Miryam and glad to learn she would soon be their stepmother. How was he going to break this news to them? What would he say?

Nothing tonight, he decided. It was too soon. He needed a night or two to think and pray and get used to the end of this particular dream. He was surprised to realize how he had gotten used to the idea of marrying Miryam, how he anticipated it, even though he had been reluctant at first. He was fond of the girl, and he had respected her. He felt anger and hurt and betrayal, but most of all he felt sadness.

It would be some time before Miryam's condition became public. He would have time to think, to decide how best to break the betrothal.

For three days Yosef buried himself in work, trying not to think about Miryam, though her face seemed always to hover in his mind's eye. The hardest part was turning aside Rahel's questions, for his curious sister quickly sensed that something was wrong and began needling him with inquiries about his bride-to-be and their wedding plans. Then, when he met her questions only with silence, she had more questions. Finally he snapped at her and told her to give him a few minutes' peace.

She did not mention Miryam's name again until that evening, when Rahel and Avram's oldest daughter returned from filling the family's water jars at the village well. As Yosef ate his evening meal he noticed the girl drawing her mother aside in the cooking area. They whispered eagerly, both darting glances in his direction. His heart felt like a stone in his chest. Had some gossip about Miryam's condition leaked out already? Or had Miryam herself begun talking to the other young women about angels and prophecies?

Neither, it seemed. Rahel, with unaccustomed gentleness, came to him later that evening as he sat sharpening a knife beside the low-burning embers of the fire. She paused in sweeping the courtyard and squatted down beside him on the ground.

"Brother, whatever the burden is you're bearing, you must stop bearing it alone. Tell me what happened between yourself and Miryam."

"There is nothing to tell," Yosef said heavily.

"I know that's not true. Your betrothed has left the village, gone away without a word to anyone. You can't tell me there's nothing wrong."

"She has done what? Gone away? But where?"

"So, you didn't know, then."

He shook his head slowly. Finally he said, "You are right. There was—trouble between us. I was going to break the betrothal. But I knew nothing of her going away. Do you know where she has gone?"

"According to what Rivkah heard at the well, nobody knows anything but that she has gone. Her parents are being very close-mouthed. Perhaps if you went to them and asked them . . ."

He didn't want to go. After the awkward and painful scenes he had endured there he never wished to enter that courtyard again. But he lay awake that night tormented by the thought of Miryam. He couldn't rest without knowing where she was. For two more days he restrained himself, but finally he went to her parents' house.

Eli did not invite Yosef into the courtyard, but stood in the entrance of the house. "Yes, my daughter has gone to stay with relatives," he said simply. His eyes, his voice, his stance didn't invite any further conversation, but Yosef couldn't leave it at that.

"Where has she gone? Have you sent her away to have the child?" It was, perhaps, an act of kindness, to spare Miryam the shame she would surely encounter in the village. And she need not be there when Yosef announced the end of their betrothal.

"We have not sent her. She chose to go, though her mother and I felt it was a wise choice. She has gone to my cousin Zechariah, who lives in the hill country of Judea."

"Judea!" So she had left not just Nazareth but Galilee altogether. *I will never see her again,* Yosef thought with a pang.

"We received a letter from my cousin—a very strange letter," Eli said, his attitude softening a little. Yosef felt the older man was still suspicious of him, but perhaps thought he was owed an explanation. "Zechariah's wife, Elisheva, is having a child. It is—unexpected. She was barren, like my Hannah, but the Lord did not bless them, and she is now quite old. They had given up hope. Zechariah is a priest, and in his letter he claimed that an angel appeared to him and told him his wife was to bear him a child." Eli shook his head. "As a sign of the Lord's power, the angel struck him dumb until the child should be born."

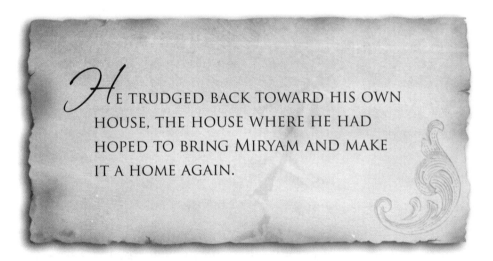

HE TRUDGED BACK TOWARD HIS OWN HOUSE, THE HOUSE WHERE HE HAD HOPED TO BRING MIRYAM AND MAKE IT A HOME AGAIN.

It was a warm, sunny day, but a chill shiver shuddered up Yosef's spine. Another story of an angel and a miraculous birth—within a few months, within the same family. But Miryam had certainly spun her story before she ever heard this tale of Zechariah and Elisheva. What could it mean? It was more than strange.

"As soon as I read the letter aloud," Eli continued, "Miryam was convinced it was another sign from God, a sign confirming what she had told us. She begged us to allow her to go visit Elisheva, and though it is a long journey, we thought it best that she be away from home at this time. I sent her off yesterday with a family passing through on their way to Jerusalem."

Yosef let out a breath he didn't even know he had been holding. "And you—what do you think of this—coincidence?" he asked. "Does it incline you to believe Miryam's tale?"

Eli shook his head slowly. "How can I believe it? The Lord performs wonders, I have no doubt of that, but to give a child to a maid with no husband? That is against the order of the world He has created. You said yourself, such things have never been spoken of among our people. Yet it is all strange, all very strange."

All very strange. That was the best conclusion Yosef himself could come up with as he trudged back toward his own house. Not Rahel's house, busy with the noises of children at work and play. No—his own, empty house. The house where he had been happy and in love with Leah, the house where he had hoped to bring Miryam and make it a home again. He went inside, took off his outer clothes, and lay down on his bed, exhausted.

Chapter Nine

MESSAGE IN THE NIGHT

Yosef awoke with a start in the middle of the night. Yet there was no sound, no one in the room. He found himself sitting upright in his bed in a dark room, with no idea why he'd awakened so suddenly.

The day that had just passed came flooding back: the news of Miryam's departure, the strange story of Zechariah and Elisheva. Yosef remembered that he was alone in the house. His children were safe with Avram and Rahel. And he was sitting here in bed, awake for no reason.

"Yosef!" A voice, clear and high as no human voice he had ever heard, pierced the silence of the room.

He twisted around, saw no one behind or beside him. Then he looked back in the direction he had first been facing, and at once shut his eyes against a brilliant light. "Yosef!" the voice called again.

"I am here! Who are you?" He put up his forearm to shield his eyes from unearthly brilliance. Peering through half-shut lids he thought he could make out a form in the light before him. Whatever it was, it was no human being, nothing he'd ever seen before.

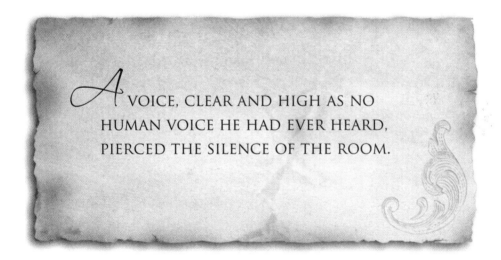

A VOICE, CLEAR AND HIGH AS NO HUMAN VOICE HE HAD EVER HEARD, PIERCED THE SILENCE OF THE ROOM.

"Do not be afraid, Yosef. I am Gabriel, the Lord's messenger. I am the same one who appeared to Miryam."

"Miryam? Did she really—wait, am I dreaming?"

"Yosef bar Yakov, carpenter of Nazareth, I have a message from the Lord," the voice said. Yosef still couldn't look directly at the form shimmering before him; it was like looking into the sun. Yet he couldn't completely shut his eyes or look away either. He was drawn to try to see.

"What message?" he gasped. "Is it about Miryam?"

"Do not fear to take Miryam as your wife. She is with child, as she has told you, but she has not betrayed you. The child within her is the child of the Holy Spirit. He will be named Yeshua, for He will save His people from their sin."

As suddenly as the vision and voice had come, it disappeared. Yosef was left alone in the dark in an empty room, with incredible words ringing in his ears. "Wait! Stay! Tell me more!" he cried into emptiness.

But there was no reply.

He didn't remember lying down, closing his eyes. All he knew was opening them again, waking in the light of dawn, knowing he had slept deeply and had a strange dream.

But as he sat up in bed, the dream came back to him. He remembered the voice, the brilliant light. The being in his room that had claimed to be an angel of the Lord, the same that had visited Miryam. And the message. Oh yes, he remembered the message.

He rose, washed, dressed, looked in his kitchen for food and found nothing there. He remembered, as if returning from a long journey, that he had not slept here in several days, that his children and his meals were waiting over the hill at Rahel's house. Would the angel have come to him if he'd stayed at Rahel's last night? Or could he only see the vision here, in his own home?

An angel; a vision. He felt sure of it, now, as he headed out into his work yard to begin the day's work. He could dismiss it as only a dream, but everything felt different, as if his life had been touched by something outside the everyday. As if he had really been in the presence of God.

This must be what she felt, he realized. *Miryam*. He remembered the certainty in her eyes, that certainty she clung to even when her parents and Yosef himself had told her

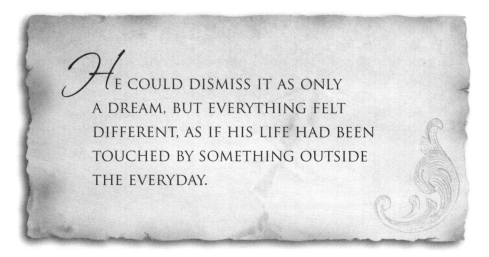

He COULD DISMISS IT AS ONLY A DREAM, BUT EVERYTHING FELT DIFFERENT, AS IF HIS LIFE HAD BEEN TOUCHED BY SOMETHING OUTSIDE THE EVERYDAY.

she was mad or lying. She had known what it felt like to be in God's presence, and she had not been able to deny that experience.

All day, as he shaped and planed and nailed wood, the memory kept humming in his mind. He could still see the brilliant light, hear the words in his head. *Do not fear to take Miryam as your wife.* A message from God telling him that Miryam had been right all along. *The child within her is of the Holy Spirit.* And even a name for the child—*Yeshua*. The Deliverer who would lead His people, just as Yeshua of old had led them across the Jordan into this promised land.

By noon Yosef was hungry, but he felt a strange reluctance to go to Rahel and Avram's house. He thought he understood why. Once he was around other people again, once he was forced to talk and act as if everything were normal, his life would start to become normal again. The dream, his sense of God's presence, would subside.

He would begin to question and doubt, to tell himself, *It was only a dream. You dreamed what you wanted to hear.* And he wasn't ready to face those doubts yet.

"Abba?"

He turned toward the small voice and saw Yakov standing at the edge of the courtyard. Not too many weeks ago, the boy would have just crossed the courtyard, picked up a plane or a hammer and begun working alongside his father without a word. Now he hesitated, as if not sure whether he still belonged there. Yosef realized

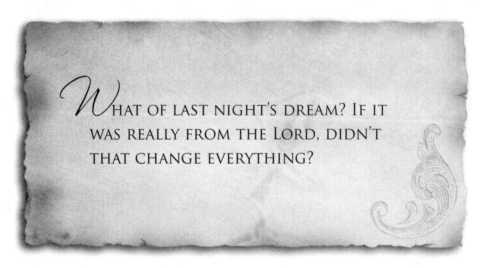

WHAT OF LAST NIGHT'S DREAM? IF IT WAS REALLY FROM THE LORD, DIDN'T THAT CHANGE EVERYTHING?

that in the weeks of his betrothal to Miryam, and even more in these last few weeks of confusion and betrayal, he had spent little time with his children, especially with this eldest son who seemed to need him more than the others.

"Come, Yakov. I was just wishing you were here to help me."

"You could have come to get me," the boy said as he came toward his father. "You didn't come home—I mean, to Uncle Avram's house last night."

"No, I didn't. I came home—here, to our home, instead. I had many things on my mind, and I slept here and had a dream that troubled me, so I have been working alone and thinking all day. But I am glad you are here now."

Yakov set to work, the muscles in his small arms straining. "When you marry Miryam, will we all move back in here with you?" he asked at last.

"Of course!" Yosef said without thinking. "You wouldn't think I would ever leave you and your brother and sisters behind, would you?"

Yakov shrugged. "Auntie said you might. That you and Miryam would want to be on your own, have a baby, start a new family."

"We might want to do all those things, but not without you!" Yosef assured his son, then stopped short, realizing he was talking as if he were still planning to marry Miryam. He would have to tell the children that she had gone away, that the betrothal was broken. But . . . what of last night's dream? If it was really from the Lord, didn't that change everything?

It changes how I feel, he thought. At least, as long as he could believe it, as long as he could hold to the memory of that moment and believe it was really the Lord's angel and not just his own weary mind that had sent that message. But Miryam was still traveling away from Nazareth, on her way to Judea.

"We do not yet know what the future may hold, my son," he said now to Yakov. "Miryam has gone away for a little time, to visit a kinswoman who is having a baby. So we will not be marrying very soon. Are you content to go on living at your aunt and uncle's house until then?"

"As long as you are there with us," Yakov said.

D ays, then weeks, passed. Yosef still turned the dream and its message over and over in his mind. He prayed for another vision, a second showing to make him more certain of the first, but nothing more was granted. *I am a new Gideon,* he thought, *putting out fleeces, asking for signs, when the Lord has already sent me an angel.* And the Lord had not called him to lead an army into battle or do any heroic deed like Gideon's—only to marry a good, devout woman and lend his name to a child that was not his own. Only that one small thing.

Some mornings he woke feeling certain. Though no more dreams came in the night, morning would find him sure that the vision had been truly from the Lord, that Miryam's child was divine and she herself blameless, that his path was clear. But in the harsh light of day that certainty ebbed. Surrounded by wood and tools, neighbors and customers, it was harder to believe in angelic messages and miraculous births.

Yosef wished he had someone to talk to about his dream and his dilemma. But who? He thought of going back to Eli and Hannah to tell them of his dream. But he knew they still half-suspected him of dishonoring their daughter. They might not believe his

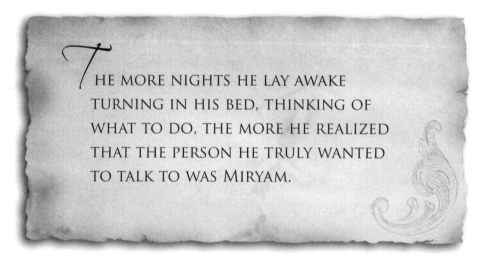

THE MORE NIGHTS HE LAY AWAKE TURNING IN HIS BED, THINKING OF WHAT TO DO, THE MORE HE REALIZED THAT THE PERSON HE TRULY WANTED TO TALK TO WAS MIRYAM.

story any more than they believed Miryam's. As for his own family—he couldn't imagine discussing this with Avram and Rahel. Rahel was already burning with curiosity to know why Miryam had left the village so abruptly and whether the marriage was going ahead, but Yosef refused to confide in her. He loved his sister, but she was a gossip. And he could not tell Avram without risking the possibility Avram might tell Rahel.

So he was alone, alone with a decision to make. The more he thought about the more nights he lay awake turning in his bed, thinking of what to do, the more he realized that the person he truly wanted to talk to was Miryam.

If only she were still in Nazareth. If only he could talk to her, tell her honestly what he had seen in the vision and the doubts and questions he'd had since. If only he could be completely certain of getting that same absolute honesty from her.

But that was the trouble, wasn't it? He couldn't be certain. He didn't know if he could trust the woman he was pledged to marry.

One Shabbat morning as he bowed his head in the synagogue, he reached out once more to God. *Please, Maker of the Universe, make my way clear to me. Should I trust in the visions— my own, and the one Miryam claims she had—and marry her, raise this child Yeshua as my own?*

Two visions, Yosef. What more do you ask?

But if I am mistaken, Lord God—I will have allowed this woman to make a fool of me.

And suddenly, amid the sonorous tones of men praying, it seemed he could hear the laughter of the Almighty. *Is that all, Yosef bar Yakov? Is that the worst that will happen—that you will look a fool? May the heavens tremble!*

He had his answer, then. No more angels, no wet fleeces. Just a sure knowledge he could carry within him like a steady flame. *What is the worst that can happen? I, Yosef the carpenter, will look like a fool. And a good girl will have a father for her fatherless child.*

I will do it, he told himself as he returned to the busy, noisy bustle of Rahel's courtyard. *I will marry the girl, and claim this child. If my dream was only a dream, then yes, it is true she has betrayed and deceived me. But she needs a husband, and a father for her child, and I will be that man. People will count the months from our marriage till the child's birth, and think I took advantage of her, dishonored her before our wedding day, nothing worse. I will bear her shame for her; they will blame me.*

And if the dream was true . . . then Yosef could not even imagine what that might mean. But he was willing to find out.

Chapter Ten

THE LETTER

With his mind at last made up, Yosef faced just one problem: his betrothed was far away, in the Judean hills, with no way of knowing what he had decided. And a busy carpenter with children to feed could not simply chase off to Judea in search of a girl, no matter how romantic such a thing might be in old tales. *Maybe the Lord will send Miryam another angel to tell her to come home,* he thought.

But he couldn't rely on that. Angels had done enough of the work in this business already. It was time for the hand of man.

Yosef could read a little, though not as well as he suspected Miryam could. The kinsman with whom she was staying was a priest, so if he sent a letter, there was no doubt that either she could read it or someone could read it to her. But he didn't trust himself to write a letter—not one that would say all he needed to say. He could read a little of the Scriptures, but beyond signing his name, he had had no need to write much. He would have to hire a scribe.

He still didn't want to confide in anyone, but a scribe was safer than any neighbor or confidant would be. Scribes were paid not just for their skill in writing, but also for their discretion. Private matters could be entrusted to a letter, and the scribe would consider it a matter of professional honor to keep the letter's contents a secret.

Even so, he didn't want to take his business to one of the two scribes in the village. Everyone in a place like Nazareth was related: through blood-ties or business-ties or close friendship. He couldn't risk the possibility that the content of his letter to Miryam might somehow, accidentally, get slipped into conversation. The whole incident required the greatest secrecy.

So he went to Sepphoris—not unusual. He had often gone to the bustling city for work. Many Galilean Jews considered the city an unclean place. It was a city full of Gentiles, ruled by the half-Gentile tetrarch, Herod. But he found, in a backstreet, a Jewish scribe who could write a letter in Aramaic. After laying down far more coins than he felt fair or necessary for the simple task, Yosef sat across a table in the scribe's small room and dictated the words he had been turning over and over in his mind for days.

My dear Miryam,

May the blessings of our Lord God be with you, my intended wife. You will see from this greeting that I have not broken my contract of betrothal, nor will I, unless you wish it. Though the story you tell still seems strange to me, it seems less strange now, for in a dream I, too, saw an angel and received a message from the Lord. This dream has assured me that I must be at peace about our marriage and its issue. I will gladly take upon myself any shame or doubt so that I can make you my wife and obey the will of God. Please return home so that we may be married as soon as possible.

Your devoted husband,
Yosef bar Yakov

When the scribe read back the words, Yosef flinched at their cold sound. He did not want to be too specific in a letter that would be seen by other eyes, that Miryam's cousin might well have to read aloud to her. He did not want to mention the child, but his meaning would be clear to her. He could not put flowery terms of affection into cold words inscribed upon paper, but he signed himself "your husband" as if the marriage were already done. No matter what he might think about this latest, strange business, he knew Miryam to be a clear-headed and rational young woman. Everything she needed to know to make a choice would be here in this letter. If she wanted to proceed with the marriage, she had only to return to Nazareth; if she chose otherwise, she would stay in Judea.

All he had to do was wait.

He took the letter from the scribe, bound and sealed, and asked around Sepphoris till he found a group of travelers headed in the right direction. Before leaving Nazareth he had already approached Eli, telling him that he wished to send a message to Miryam. Eli had seemed guarded and wary, but he gave Yosef the full name of his cousin and the village where he lived—information Yosef now passed on to the travelers, parting with a few more coins in return for their promise to deliver the letter.

Everything she needed to know to make a choice would be here in this letter. If she wanted to proceed with the marriage, she had only to return to Nazareth; if she chose otherwise, she would stay in Judea.

He retraced his steps that evening—a whole day's work and earning lost, and money spent in the bargain, on a letter he could not even be sure would reach Miryam. And if it did? He tried to picture her opening it. In his mind's eye he saw her dark hair and eyes, her serious mouth, her slender form. Still slender? Would the child in her womb be beginning to show by now?

What would she think, as she read those words, or as a learned cousin read them aloud? In his imagination he tried to see what lay behind her eyes, but as ever since this business began, he could not be sure. It all depended on the truth—the truth only Miryam could ever know for sure. If the child was the child of another man, if she were deceiving him, she might feel relief, or triumph, or even contempt at how she'd deceived him. But relief, most likely—that someone was willing to marry her, to take her stained reputation and attach it to his own flawless one.

And if she told the truth? If her vision, and his own dream, were really of God? That was the unlikely possibility on which Yosef was staking his future, and yet he couldn't really grasp it, couldn't imagine what it might mean. That the Almighty in-

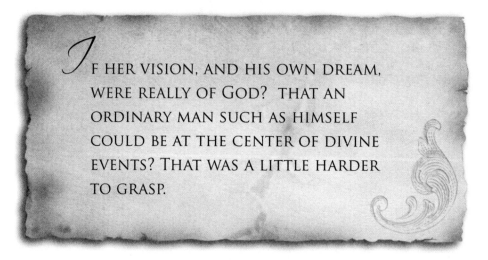

If her vision, and his own dream, were really of God? That an ordinary man such as himself could be at the center of divine events? That was a little harder to grasp.

volved Himself in the affairs of humble men and women—this he knew from the Scriptures. But that he, Yosef, a carpenter of Nazareth in the conquered land of Galilee in the reign of Caesar Augustus—that an ordinary man such as himself could be at the center of divine events? That was a little harder to grasp.

He pushed it to the back of his mind, tried to immerse himself in daily chores, in his work, in caring for his children who were still living at Avram and Rahel's, as he was himself. He had had to sternly order Rahel to ask no more questions about Miryam. Sternly enough that, for once, his sister actually obeyed.

Underneath all his busyness there was simply nothing to do but wait—for a return letter, for another message from the Lord, for Miryam herself. Days passed into weeks. He couldn't stop himself from speculating about whether the letter had reached her, whether she had read it yet. Perhaps he should write again? Letters were so unreliable.

She had been gone three months, and his letter nearly two, when Yosef's wait finally ended. He was in his own work yard late one afternoon as the long rays of sun slanted across his workbench, making the shadows long and deep. Yakov worked beside him, and Yosef noted with pride that the boy's hands on the hammer were as sure as a man's, his blows as true. No childish fumbling here. Yakov was 11 years old now, on the threshold of adulthood.

Still, he was a boy, and boys must eat. Yosef wasn't ready to stop work himself. Another hour and he could put the job aside without it gnawing at the edges of his mind. "Yakov, you're done for the day," he announced. "They'll be serving the evening meal at your aunt and uncle's house. Go quickly and join them. Tell Aunt Rahel that I will be there a little later. She can save a bowl of stew and some bread for me."

"Are you sure, Abba? I could stay, help you finish . . ."

"No, my son. Go eat your dinner."

"Yes, Abba." Quickly the boy tidied his workspace, picked up his tunic and pulled it on again over his small bare chest, and hurried down the hill toward his aunt's home.

Yosef worked on. Perhaps it was the sound of hammer on nails, or the plane against the wood, that deafened him to other sounds. He didn't look up till a new shadow fell across his hands, across the wood.

She stood there. Miryam, wrapped in a dark cloak. He thought he might be dreaming again.

"Miryam?" he said.

"I called your name, but you were too absorbed in your work. I . . . I wasn't sure if I should come."

He laid down his tools and reached out his hands toward her. After a moment, she took them in her own. "I just arrived back in the village an hour ago," she said. "I came here first—I haven't even seen my parents yet."

"Nobody knows you're here? But—what if someone sees you, coming alone to my house?"

"What of my reputation, you mean?" She glanced down, and he could see that her stomach was softly rounded now. "My reputation is lost now, no matter what. And if you really mean what you said in your letter, yours is too. You know what people will assume—that we could not wait for our wedding day, and that you took advantage of me. Are you sure you want everyone to say that?"

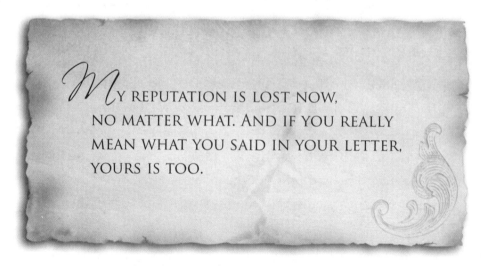

My REPUTATION IS LOST NOW, NO MATTER WHAT. AND IF YOU REALLY MEAN WHAT YOU SAID IN YOUR LETTER, YOURS IS TOO.

He nodded, still holding her hands. "I am willing to bear that."

"So—the Lord sent you a dream?"

Briefly, he recounted what he had seen and heard that night. "Yeshua," she repeated, trying out the name. "The angel said nothing to me about a name. But it is right, of course. The same thing happened to my cousin Elisheva and her husband. An angel told them their son would be called Yochannan, and they held firmly to that name, even when all the relatives and villagers had other names to suggest. You can't imagine how it strengthened my faith, to come from Nazareth where no one believed me, to go there and find they, too, had had a message from the Lord about their child."

"Yes . . . your father told me of Elisheva and her husband," Yosef said. "It made me think—made your parents think, too—that there was more to your story than we had first thought. But you must understand why—how hard it was for us to believe you . . ."

"I do. I do understand. It was hard for me to believe myself, until—well, until my own body began to tell me the truth." Miryam dropped his hands, only to launch herself unexpectedly into his arms and press her face against his shoulder. "Oh, Yosef, I'm so glad the Lord showed you the truth. So very, very glad you believe it too, now, and we can bear this burden together."

She was weeping, and despite the impropriety of it he held her, stroked her hair and comforted her. He couldn't tell her—he would never be able to tell her—that there was still a shadow of doubt in his heart, still the fear that his dream had only been what he wanted to believe, rather than a true sending from the Lord. Now that she was here, in his arms, committed once again to be his bride, he could not doubt she was telling the truth, bizarre though it was. And if she was not—if that little seed of doubt still lingered—what did it matter? It would not change what he had promised to do—to take her under his protection, to bear her shame, to raise her child. This was what the Lord had called him to do.

Of that one thing, Yosef was absolutely certain.

Chapter Eleven

THE WEDDING

Family, friends, and neighbors gathered in the courtyard of Yosef's home for the wedding feast. The workbenches, tools, and planks of wood had been cleared away for the day, replaced with long tables laden with food. Rahel and her older daughters had done everything custom demanded of a bridegroom's family and more, providing platter after platter of dishes for the guests to sample.

Everyone was merry and high-spirited, warmly congratulating the bride and groom, though Yosef couldn't help but notice the glances that the older women shot in Miryam's direction. Her condition was not yet fully apparent, but it seemed that even beneath her wedding gown some of those sharp-eyed village wives had caught a glimpse. Or perhaps it was a whisper of gossip they had caught instead?

Never mind. Yosef put those thoughts from his mind. There would be stares, and comments, and gossip to deal with in the months ahead, but this day was for celebrating. Miryam was across the courtyard from him, dancing hand in hand in a circle with a group of young girls her own age. Some were already wives, some still waiting for

EVEN BENEATH HER WEDDING GOWN
SOME OF THOSE SHARP-EYED VILLAGE
WIVES HAD CAUGHT A GLIMPSE.

their own wedding days. Yosef found his eyes drifting in that direction again and again. How easy it was to pick her out from all the other silly, giggling girls. How different she was—and not just because of her wedding finery. She danced with them but somehow apart, as though she were made of something finer— linen next to homespun cotton.

You sound like a boy in love, he told himself, and shook his head at the thought. He hadn't felt this way since—well, since Leah. Her presence lurked in the background of this wedding day—every moment matched to the memory of that other wedding day 12 years earlier. He caught glimpses of Leah in the faces of her children and hoped that, if she could have known, she would be happy for him. She had had no time to say goodbye to him, but surely she would have wished him not just a housekeeper and a mother for the children but—a new life, even a new love.

But Leah's imagined presence was never stronger than when the tables were cleared and the guests had gone. Even the children were gone with Rahel and Avram one last time, after bidding goodnight—a warm and affectionate goodnight in the case of the younger children, a solemn one in Yakov's case—to their father and new stepmother. Tomorrow they would return to live in their own home again, but tonight, just for tonight this house was Yosef and Miryam's alone.

But it could never be that, never theirs alone. He cursed the memories he couldn't shake off, but it was, always would be, Leah's house, the home he had shared with his first bride. And another presence haunted them as well—the unborn child, the child who was not his, waiting inside Miryam's womb to change everything.

They did not speak of either of those unseen presences, but sat across the table from each other in the main room of the house, looking at each other with the wary shyness of a new husband and wife truly alone together for the first time.

Yosef reached out and placed his hand on the table, palm up. After a moment, Miryam placed her hand in his. "You look tired," he said.

Her face fell a little, and he could have kicked himself. A girl wants to look beautiful on her bridal day, not tired. "Lovely, but tired," he amended. "It has been a long day."

"I am tired," Miryam said. "I often am, these days. Elisheva said it's to be expected when I'm with child. I wish I could talk to some of the other women about it but—"

"You can talk to me," Yosef said. "It's our secret, remember? You can tell me anything. And remember, I'm an old widower. I know a little about women and child-bearing. I know enough to let you sit and put your feet up when you're tired, to let you rest a little longer in bed in the mornings. Things of that sort."

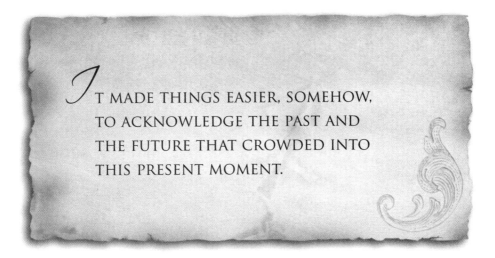

IT MADE THINGS EASIER, SOMEHOW, TO ACKNOWLEDGE THE PAST AND THE FUTURE THAT CROWDED INTO THIS PRESENT MOMENT.

There. In a way, now, both their ghosts had been raised and spoken of: Leah and the baby. It made things easier, somehow, to acknowledge the past and the future that crowded into this present moment. But there was another worry, and Yosef saw it in Miryam's shadowed eyes. He would have to put her mind at rest.

"You are wondering if I'll insist on sharing your bed right away," he said.

She looked down, embarrassed, then raised her eyes to meet his full-on—the glance that he was coming to think of as essentially hers, the thing that made her Miryam. Things might surprise or daunt her for a moment, but they would never make her flinch or drop her clear-eyed gaze for long. She looked at the world straight-on, this girl, and it was that quality, more than anything else, that he had come to cherish about her. No need to mince words or play games with Miryam.

"You are a beautiful woman, my bride, and I long to take you in my arms and know you as a husband knows his wife," Yosef said. "But you are with child, and still half a stranger to me. Perhaps it's best if we use these months while you carry the child to become friends before being lovers? You are welcome to sleep in my bed, and I will sleep beside you with you in my arms if you wish, or in another bed if you prefer. We can take our time."

She looked relieved. He saw her little sigh before her face lifted to his again. "I am very grateful, Yosef. Not because I don't desire to be a true wife to you, nor because I'm afraid but because—this baby I carry—well, it's something special. I don't fully understand, but . . . I want to be careful."

"Yes." Actually, at this very moment he had a great desire to take her in his arms and kiss her. And hadn't he just thought that she was a girl with whom he could always be honest, always be direct? So perhaps that was all right. "What about a kiss?" he asked. "Is that careful enough?"

She rose from her seat and came to stand before him. "I think a kiss would be—very suitable, my husband." For the first time that day he saw her radiant smile, and it dazzled him as he took her into his arms.

Chapter Twelve

THE CENSUS

The days of late summer unrolled like fine linen from a merchant's stall. Yosef marveled at how quickly his new domestic routine had established itself, how smoothly Miryam had fit into the pattern of their lives, and how that pattern had reshaped itself to include her. He realized that somewhere deep inside he had feared they would never become a family. He had imagined Rahel might make trouble, might insist on the children staying with her, or that they might be reluctant to leave her home which had now become familiar. Or perhaps the children would have trouble getting used to Miryam, or she would have trouble coping with them, a young girl suddenly saddled with a house, a husband, and four growing stepchildren.

But no. Until the marriage was a fact he hadn't even realized how much those fears had gnawed at the back of his mind. Now they were gone, and she was here, and he realized that the fears had been not only wordless but groundless. Under Miryam's care, the house became, as it had been when Leah was alive, a home again. She cooked, she cleaned, she wove fabric and sewed clothes for the children, as well as for the new baby. She sang softly as she went about the housework, and soon had the little girls singing too, trailing her around the house, crooning to their doll as Miryam sang to them. For them, and for Yehudah too, she seemed to be a born mother, to take to the role as naturally as if she had birthed them.

With Yakov it was more difficult, as Yosef had known it would be. The boy was polite and respectful to his stepmother, of course—as he was to everyone. But she was, after all, a mere five years his senior, and during the years since his mother's death Yakov had become accustomed to living without a mother. He had never really allowed Rahel to fill that role, and it seemed he would not let Miryam into that place in his heart either. He had become used, too, to being his father's companion and in some ways his confidant. Yosef couldn't help but notice the quiet, wary glances the boy sent in his direction in the evening as the younger children settled down to their beds and Yosef sat beside Miryam on the bench by the fire, enjoying a moment together after the hard work of the day. Yes, it would take time for Miryam to fully win Yakov's heart, and when she did, it would not be as a new mother, as she was to the younger children. But perhaps, in time, Yakov would come to love and trust her as a friend, almost an older sister. At least, that was Yosef's hope. He loved Yakov, and he loved Miryam. They were both good people, kind and sensible, even if they were wary of each other. Time would forge a bond between them, he was sure. Almost sure.

As for his own heart—well, yes. He was growing to love Miryam, just as he'd hoped he would once the marriage was made. And slowly, he noticed that his constant habit of comparing her to Leah—her low chuckle to Leah's rowdy laugh, her lullabies to the ones Leah had sung, even her bread to Leah's—had begun to drop away. He was beginning to love her for herself, Miryam, his second wife, instead of thinking always of her as Leah's replacement.

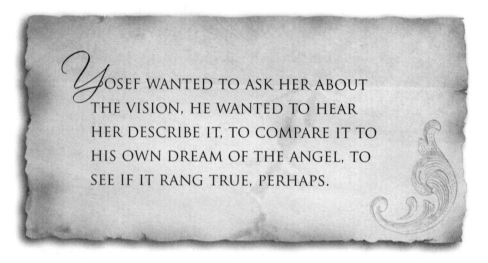

YOSEF WANTED TO ASK HER ABOUT THE VISION, HE WANTED TO HEAR HER DESCRIBE IT, TO COMPARE IT TO HIS OWN DREAM OF THE ANGEL, TO SEE IF IT RANG TRUE, PERHAPS.

But the baby. Well, that was a complication. Miryam's pregnancy was obvious by now, and it put their marriage on a different footing from the start. With the baby on the way, and the strange story of its conception that, despite everything, Yosef still couldn't fully believe or understand, there was no question of them starting out as an ordinary married couple. It was as if their true marriage was waiting, held in abeyance, until after the baby's birth. Until then, things still felt unsettled and unsure, despite the newfound domestic peace and happiness that Miryam brought to the little house.

They didn't talk much about the baby. Yosef wanted to ask her about the vision, about the angel, but something held him back. He needed to hear the story, for when she'd tried to tell him first, he hadn't really been listening. Like her parents, he had been looking past the story, for the true explanation. Now he wanted to hear her describe it, to compare it to his own dream of the angel, to see if it rang true, perhaps. But he could never bring himself to frame the question. The whole topic of the baby hung between them like an uneasy secret, something they were both aware of but never discussed.

One morning as he worked in the yard, Miryam returned from drawing water at the village well. Shirah and Yehudah trotted by her side, Yehudah carrying one of the water jars. Little Leah rode at Miryam's hip, while she balanced the other water jar on her opposite hip. Yehudah went into the house with Miryam and Leah, while Shirah came over to watch Yosef and Yakov at work.

"Miryam's sad, Abba," the girl said.

"She is?" She hadn't looked particularly sad when she came back from the well, but then, he hadn't really been paying attention. "Why is she sad?"

"I don't know. Some women were talking, at the well. She didn't talk to them, but she listened, and it made her sad. I think that was it, anyway. I asked her about it, but she wouldn't say."

As soon as Yosef was able to take a few minutes' break from his work, he went into the kitchen to find Miryam. She was kneading bread dough, her head bent low over her work. The children were playing outside, so he was alone as he put an arm around her waist and said, "Shirah said you were sad . . . something that someone said at the well made you sad."

She gave her head a tiny shake. "It's nothing. I'm sorry I let Shirah see I was troubled—I shouldn't let it bother me."

"Tell me."

"No."

"Please, Miryam." Still holding her, he felt her movements slow, her hands stop kneading the dough, and then she turned and pressed her face against his shoulder, against his bare sun-warmed skin, for he worked stripped to the waist as always.

"It's only gossip. I should not listen," she said. "I knew—I expected this."

"Who was it? What did they say?"

She shook her head again, pressed her lips together, but the words came out as if she couldn't restrain them. "Just—some women. Neighbors. I won't say who. One asked me when the baby was coming, and I said late in the autumn. Then they turned to each other and started talking. One said—she said she never thought Yosef the carpenter was that sort of man, and the other said I must have led you astray, that such a sin was often the fault of a wayward girl. Then another said, Yes, if Yosef even is the father. They spoke loudly enough—they meant me to hear, even though they weren't speaking to me. My poor mother—you wouldn't believe the things women have said to her, pretending to comfort her, but really trying to hurt, to make her say something against me."

Yosef held her close and stroked her hair. "I'm sorry, so sorry you must go through this."

"You're going through it too. Your good name is being dragged through the mud."

He tipped her face up to meet his. "It would be worse for you, if you were alone, you know."

"I know that, of course!" She looked almost angry. "And I'm grateful. But if we hadn't married, I'd be far away from here, and the gossips would be strangers to me. It's harder, somehow, when they're women I've known all my life. Friends of my mother, mothers of my friends. Even some of my own friends turn away from me now, as if they're ashamed to be seen talking to me."

"Oh, Miryam. My Miryam." He didn't know what else to say, so he just held her and continued to caress her long, dark hair. He knew that no words of his could make it right, and that both of them would have to endure much in the way of scorn and criticism. "Perhaps this is part of the burden the Lord has asked us to bear. If your child truly is—special, as you say—if He is going to be the Lord's Anointed, Israel's Deliverer, then our lives will not be ordinary, will they? Gossip and unkind comments at the village well will be the least of what you may have to bear." She turned her eyes, shiny with unshed tears, up to him, and he saw that he had said exactly the right thing, at last. She could bear any hardship, if she believed it came from the hand of God, if it was part of the special task He had called her to. "But I promise you," Yosef went on, "that whatever the trouble, I will stand beside you through it all. You will never be alone."

High voices and small running feet interrupted them. The children had come back inside, and Yosef and Miryam quickly pulled apart as she returned to her bread dough.

He thought all day about the scene at the village well, wondering if there was anything he could do to minimize the effect of the town's gossip. Rahel was his obvious ally, of course, and though normally she was the first to start wagging her tongue, she had said nothing at all about Miryam's pregnancy. He wondered what his sister thought. Did she assume the child was Yosef's, or that of some other man? Whatever she thought, Rahel, though a busybody, had a good heart. And she was fiercely loyal. Yosef decided he would draw her aside for a quiet talk, ask her to use her influence among the other women to make things easier for Miryam and her mother. *I married her to protect her and the child,* Yosef thought, *and this is one thing I can do. Rahel will help, even if she doesn't understand—and even if the fact that she doesn't understand drives her mad.*

Those thoughts were still in his mind a few hours later when Yosef saw his brother-in-law Avram standing at the entrance to his courtyard. "Avram, my brother, come in," Yosef said. It was rare for his busy brother-in-law to take even a few moments away from his own work and household. He relied on Rahel to come and go with news of the outside world for him. "Come in, have a seat. Miryam, can you bring a drink for Avram?" He guided his visitor to a bench in the shade.

"Have you heard the news?" Avram asked, without preliminaries.

Yosef's heart fell. Had the women's gossip about Miryam and himself become so vicious that it required Avram to speak to him, man to man? "What news?" he asked, bracing himself.

"The news of the census."

"The . . . census?"

Avram turned his head and spat upon the ground. "The Romans," he said. "They are raising a new tax—of course—and they have ordered there be a census. Everyone is to register so we can all be taxed again and again to pay for Rome's legions and for Caesar's throne."

Yosef shrugged. "So it is, and so it will ever be until the Messiah comes to set us free." He felt a strange chill, saying those words, holding the secret knowledge. Could it really be true—of Miryam's child, and what the angel had promised? Could this child, now sleeping in Miryam's womb, someday set the chosen people free from Caesar's iron grip, drive out the legions, and establish Israel as a nation again, with its own king on the throne? "Until then, we register, and we pay taxes. Not that we're not paying enough, already."

"This one is different," Avram said. "Every man goes to register, not in the town where he lives now, but in the town where he was born, where his family line comes from. You know what that means for you, for people like you?"

People like you. Avram's family, like many people in the village, had lived in the same area for generations, never travelling far from the place their fathers and grandfathers had been born. But not everyone was like that. Yosef's father had come north to Galilee as a young married man with two little children, Yosef and Rahel. His family was from Judea, from the village of Bethlehem, outside Jerusalem. He had been proud of his heritage, old Yakov had—he could trace his lineage all the way back to the sons of King David.

Yosef had never given much thought, one way or another, to that ancient family line stretching back to Bethlehem. Certainly he had never expected to go back to his birthplace.

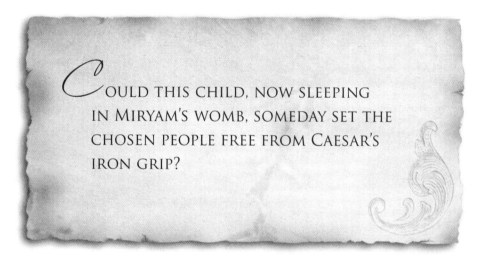

COULD THIS CHILD, NOW SLEEPING IN MIRYAM'S WOMB, SOMEDAY SET THE CHOSEN PEOPLE FREE FROM CAESAR'S IRON GRIP?

"What about Rahel?" he asked. "Surely women don't have to go to their family's home—they will register with their husband's families, won't they?"

"Of course," Avram said. "But the tax collectors and officials, those traitors who do Rome's work for them—they say a man must bring his whole family along, wife and children, if he's required to travel. Are you going to go to Bethlehem with four young children and a wife who is—forgive me—expecting another before too long?"

"I don't know, brother," Yosef said. He was so absorbed in thinking about the census and what it might mean that Avram's reference to Miryam's pregnancy didn't even trouble him. He tried to imagine himself taking the long road south to Bethlehem with Miryam and all the children. Then he tried to imagine leaving them behind. Either way, it was impossible.

He told Miryam about it later that night, when the children were asleep. "Do you really have to go? All the way to Bethlehem?" she said.

"I could try to avoid it, hope the authorities never find out I came from Bethlehem," he admitted. "But I don't want to make trouble. I'm a law-abiding man, even when I don't agree with the laws. If it weren't for you and the children, I wouldn't even hesitate about going."

"If you believe it's right, then of course we must go," Miryam said.

"We?"

"I won't be left behind, without you."

He thought of the women at the village well. "Perhaps it is best if you come with me," he said thoughtfully. Ridiculous and disruptive as this taxation census might be, it could be a godsend—literally—for Miryam. Leaving Nazareth at this time, settling, at least temporarily, in a village where no one knew her as anything other than Yosef's wife, or had any reason to suspect the baby had not been conceived in their marriage bed. *Yes, that would be a welcome relief for Miryam just now,* he thought.

"What about the children?" he wondered aloud. "Perhaps Rahel and Avram will keep them. It would be a long and wearying journey for them, and surely it's not necessary they come, is it?" It would be good for him and Miryam to have the time to themselves, to accustom themselves to being married without the pressure of having the children to care for as well. Perhaps they could travel to Bethlehem, stay there till the baby was born, and when he was old enough to travel, return to Nazareth.

"It would be too long, for them to be away from you," Miryam said. "Who knows what might happen, once we're in Judea? It may be better to bring them along."

He guessed, then, that she was thinking of staying in Bethlehem, thinking that Yosef might choose to settle in his ancestral home and not return to Nazareth. And he had to admit, the idea did have a certain appeal. A fresh start for all of them. Far from family and friends in Nazareth, it was true, but also far from gossip and suspicion. Well, if that were to be even a possibility, he would have to go to Bethlehem with the tools of his trade, four young children, and a very pregnant wife. It was no light undertaking.

"I wonder if this, too, is all part of the Lord's plan," he mused aloud.

"It is, Yosef, I'm sure of it. I want this baby to be born in Bethlehem."

"Why? I do understand why you want to leave here, but why Bethlehem?"

"There's something in the Scriptures—in the Prophets, I'm sure—about Bethlehem. I have to find the scrolls, to see if I remember it right."

Yosef thought of the Scripture readings he'd heard over the years of attending the synagogue. He remembered nothing special about Bethlehem save that it was the home of King David, but he knew that though Miryam was only a woman, her knowledge of Scripture—and even her ability to read it for herself—was greater than his.

He was tired now, as much from the thought of what the months ahead would hold as from this day's work. He rolled over on his side in the bed, ready for sleep. "When you learn why Bethlehem matters so much, be sure to tell me," was the last thing he said before he closed his eyes and slept.

Chapter Thirteen

ISRAEL'S DELIVERER

Sunset fell on the day of Preparation. Yosef's work was laid aside for the Shabbat, his hammer and axe stilled for a day. The children, freshly washed and dressed in clean clothes, gathered around for the Shabbat meal while Miryam lit a lamp to welcome the sacred hours.

What a joy it was, to again have a wife and mother in the house to welcome Shabbat! In the years since Leah's death, even when Yosef and the children had been living in their own home, they had always gone to Rahel and Avram's house to eat the Shabbat meal. It was a family celebration, hollow and empty in a house without a matriarch.

Miryam filled the role as if she had been waiting all her life to do this, to preside as wife and mother, saying the Shabbat prayer as the glow of lamplight filled the little house. Her face glowed, too, as her eyes met his over the heads of the children.

As they were eating, she said, "Tomorrow, after we worship in the synagogue, stay behind with me. My father will meet us there. He has spoken to the rabbi about allowing us to look at some of the scrolls."

Yosef knew that Miryam's father had, for a common working man, a keen knowledge of the Scriptures and the ability to read well. In fact, Eli owned a scroll of the psalms, an unusual thing for a villager to possess. Miryam had learned to read from that scroll, and had been an avid listener from beyond the women's wall in the synagogue, her quick mind drinking up all she heard.

This urgent request must have something to do with Bethlehem, Yosef realized. Since news of the taxation and census had come a few weeks ago, Miryam had latched eagerly on to the idea. For some reason, traveling to Bethlehem—surely not an appealing prospect for most young women in her condition—had captured her imagination, and he knew it was more than just the chance to escape the prying eyes and wagging tongues of Nazareth's women. Bethlehem, itself, held some appeal he couldn't quite grasp, and she herself had told him it had something to do with the Scriptures.

So the next day, after the service, he stayed behind with Miryam and her father. The rabbi, too, was curious to know why this woman so badly wanted to find a particular passage of Scripture.

"It is somewhere in the Prophets—one of the minor ones, I think," Eli said to the rabbi, darting quick glances at Miryam for confirmation. It would not be appropriate for her to speak in such a setting. Her father or husband must speak to the rabbi for her, but it was clear to all three men who was the driving force behind this meeting, who was so anxious to dive into the dusty old scrolls. "A prophecy about Bethlehem, about the Messiah."

"Ah. Ah yes," the rabbi said, and shuffled over to the collection of scrolls, drawing forth first one and then another. "Joel, I think." He unrolled a scroll, ran his finger right to left across the page, tracing the letters. "H'mmm . . . no . . . wait. Micah, perhaps." He rolled up Joel's prophecy, took out another. "Here. Is this the passage you mean?"

> *But you, Bethlehem Ephrathah,*
> *though you are small among the clans of Judah,*
> *out of you will come for me*
> *one who will be ruler over Israel,*
> *whose origins are from of old,*
> *from ancient times.*

Eli nodded slowly, then looked to Miryam. Her dark eyes were bright and expectant, and she leaned closer to her father to speak. "My daughter—she wishes to read the words for herself," Eli said, as if half-embarrassed, then glanced at Yosef. "If it is all right with her husband."

"Of course, of course," Yosef said, wishing he could read better himself. The rabbi, a little put out but also intrigued by the strange procedure, stepped aside to allow Miryam to see the scroll. He still held it in place himself, though, as if unwilling to let a woman's hand touch the sacred parchment.

Yes, it would be nice to read the Scriptures for himself, Yosef thought as he watched

Miryam whisper the words, but he didn't need to read the scroll in order to know what was in her mind. This explained why, rather than being daunted by the thought of Bethlehem, she was eager to make the trip. *"Out of you will come . . . one who will be ruler over Israel."* She believed the child she carried was Israel's Deliverer, and this

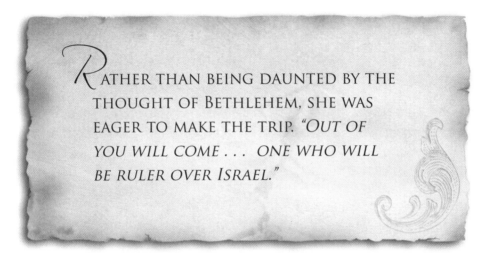

Rather than being daunted by the thought of Bethlehem, she was eager to make the trip. "Out of you will come . . . one who will be ruler over Israel."

prophecy promised that the Anointed One would be born in Bethlehem.

"There is another," Miryam said, forgetting her place and speaking for herself, directly to the rabbi. "Something from the prophet Isaiah—about the Anointed One coming from the line of Jesse and David."

The rabbi frowned, but he too was intrigued, and pulled the Isaiah scroll from the clay pot where it rested. After a few moments he read aloud again:

> *A shoot will come up from the stump of Jesse;*
> *from his roots a Branch will bear fruit.*
> *The Spirit of the Lord will rest on him—*
> *the Spirit of wisdom and of understanding,*
> *the Spirit of counsel and of power,*

the Spirit of knowledge and of the fear of the Lord—
and he will delight in the fear of the Lord.
He will not judge by what he sees with his eyes,
or decide by what he hears with his ears;
but with righteousness he will judge the needy,
with justice he will give decisions for the poor of the earth.

That afternoon, while the children played quietly in the corners of the courtyard, Miryam and Yosef sat with Eli and Hannah, talking of the prophecies that so intrigued Miryam.

"You see how it all fits?" she said, her eyes still glittering with that strange enthusiasm. "The angel told me and told Yosef that the child would be the Deliverer. The prophet says the Lord's Anointed will come from Bethlehem, and before my child is due to be born, my husband receives an order to return to Bethlehem! Because he is of the house of David—as are we!" she added, turning to her parents. "The Messiah will come from the house of David, in the town of David. Don't you see? The prophets foretold it all!"

Yosef was torn. Half of him was caught up in her excitement, wanting to believe all that she believed. The other half was more cautious, hearing in her talk of angels and messiahs the delusions of a devout girl who wanted desperately to believe that the child she carried was important, was a child of destiny. He saw that same doubt reflected in the eyes of Miryam's parents as the girl leaned forward, eager to convince them.

But he knew the one thing that Eli and Hannah could never know for certain— Miryam's child was definitely not his. And the more he got to know his new wife, the more impossible it seemed that she could ever have deceived him. And if that was so, then the baby was all she said it was, and the words of dusty old scrolls were far more significant than he had ever guessed. A chill touched his spine.

"True, both our family and Yosef's can trace our line back to the house of David," Eli was saying to his daughter. "But the house of David has fallen on hard times in these days, Miryam. We may have a proud lineage—so do thousands in Israel—but we are laborers and workingmen, servants in our own land. The king of Israel today—if you can call Herod a king—is not even a Jew by blood, much less of the line of David. Our real ruler is Caesar in Rome, and the house of David is more likely to produce shepherds again, than kings."

"But you've said it yourself!" Miryam insisted. "David himself was nothing but a shepherd when the Lord anointed him. The Lord can raise up whomever He chooses to accomplish His purpose. What if it is, indeed, my child He has chosen? That is what my vision told me. That is what Yosef's dream told him. Surely we should go to Bethlehem and fulfill the Lord's plan?"

"It's such a long journey, and so risky at such a time," Hannah said. She was a practical woman, and all the talk of Messiah and prophecy mattered less to her than the practical business of her pregnant daughter traveling the length of the land in the months before her child was due. "If Yosef went on alone to Bethlehem, he could go and be back more quickly. You could stay here with us, and Yosef's children could stay with his sister and brother, and all would be safe and well. He might even return before the babe is born."

"No," Miryam said, her face taking on its stubborn set. Ah, but she was a strong-willed woman, for all her quiet modesty. Yosef had already determined he would issue as few direct orders in his married life as he could manage, for he didn't want to face those eyes and that stubborn set of her mouth too often. Far better to reason and negotiate, for when Miryam's mind was set to something—like having her child born in Bethlehem—there was no shaking her.

Chapter Fourteen

IN THE HANDS OF THE LORD

So it was that one day in autumn Yosef loaded his tools and several bundles of household goods onto the back of a new-bought donkey. He'd never owned a beast before, never had need of one, but there was much to carry on this journey. Miriam and the little girls could take turns riding on the donkey's back when they were too tired to walk. Miryam was seven months into her pregnancy now.

Three months had passed since Yosef had married her. It was not a good time for a journey. It would have been better if he could have left sooner, but he had been determined to finish all the jobs he had contracted to do. He had no idea when they would return to Nazareth, if ever, and such a long and uncertain journey would require all the money he could lay hands on. So he had spent weeks of hard, backbreaking labor in preparation for the trip.

He had delayed leaving till as late in the year as he possibly could to accommodate both the census decree—which must be accomplished before the onset of winter—and Miryam's pregnancy. Later than this, they could not dream of leaving. Even now, Yosef feared the strain of the journey might bring the baby early and threaten both Miryam's survival and the child's.

But Miryam seemed to have no fear at all. The prospect of the journey buoyed and excited her, and he heard her every day talking to the children about the things they would see on the road to Bethlehem. Of course, she had covered some of this same road before, earlier in the year, on her visit to Zechariah and Elisheva. Yosef had never traveled further than Tiberias, except for that first, unremembered journey as a child younger than little Leah, when he had accompanied his parents north from Bethlehem.

Now, finally, it was the day of departure. A caravan of travelers had stopped in Nazareth the night before, and Yosef, prepared for several days now, had been awaiting just such an opportunity. He didn't want his little family to take to the roads alone, so he had arranged with the travelers—who were also going south to register for the census—to travel along with them. They would leave just after dawn, and now, in first light, Yosef tied bundles to the donkey's back while Miryam wrapped the children in traveling cloaks.

When they made their slow way to the village inn where the travelers were also preparing for departure, he wasn't surprised to see Avram and Rahel along with Miryam's parents, gathered there to say goodbye.

Yosef had had many long and difficult conversations with his sister over these last weeks. Rahel had done everything she could to dissuade him from taking Miryam and the children to Bethlehem. While he still hadn't told Rahel the strange stories and secrets surrounding Miryam's child, he had insisted that it was of utmost importance to Miryam to have her baby born far from Nazareth. "She wants to go to Bethlehem. She won't change her mind," he had explained again and again.

"Fine then. Take her, if you want to risk her life and the baby's. But leave the children with me," Rahel had said. "My house is their true home, anyway. They've hardly had time to get used to Miryam as a stepmother, and now there'll be a new baby brother or sister, and a journey to the south. It's not right to put them through all that."

She had made her plea several times, and though Yosef had been tempted to accept the offer, he had refused every time. Now, as Miryam exchanged embraces and farewells with her parents, Rahel pulled Yosef aside and tried again.

"It's not too late, brother. Leave the children with me. The little ones, anyway. Maybe Yakov won't be separated from you, but the others . . . leave them with me. By the time you get there, winter will be coming on, and the baby born—who knows when you'll return to Nazareth?"

He held her steady, his arms on her plump ones, his eyes fixed to hers. "Who knows, indeed, Rahel. Who knows? The children must come with us."

"Then it's true. Winding up your business, taking all your tools, bringing the children—you don't intend to return to Nazareth, do you, brother?"

He sighed. "I do not know what we intend, Rahel. We must be prepared. I am placing my family in the hands of the Lord. That is all I know."

"In the hands of the Lord!" She moved closer, pulling him by his sleeve till she was almost speaking in his ear. "We are all in the hands of the Lord, Yosef, but don't think I don't know of Miryam's delusions. Do you think the rabbi doesn't talk to his wife, or that she doesn't talk to other women? I know Miryam clings to some mad belief that her child will be something special, maybe the Lord's Anointed, and that she believes it must be born in Bethlehem of the house of David. So she's found

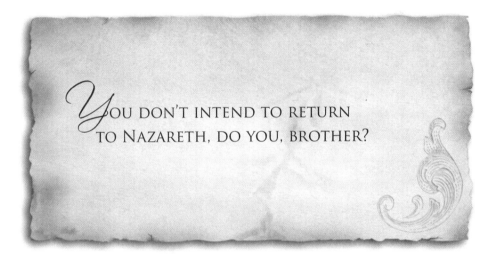

You don't intend to return to Nazareth, do you, brother?

herself a husband of David's line and a way to get to Bethlehem in time. But must you be taken in by a young girl's folly? Will you destroy your own life, and your children's lives, to cover her sin?"

"Shut your mouth, sister," Yosef said quietly but firmly. "You speak true. I do not know when we will return, if ever. You are the only living family member I have, and I would not have our parting marred by bitter words. Close your mouth and your heart against the slanders you hear about Miryam and me, and don't remember your brother as a fool. Remember me as a servant of God, and remember that His purposes may be stranger and deeper than we can comprehend."

While Rahel still stared at him, dumbstruck at his words and his unaccustomed sternness, he leaned forward and kissed her on the cheek, then turned her to face her husband, who was talking to one of the travelers about the dangers of bandits on the road south. "Avram, my brother, farewell. Continue to take good care of my sister and my nieces and nephews, and remember us in your prayers. Eli, Hannah, farewell. Yakov, Yehudah, bring your sisters and come. It's time to take to the road."

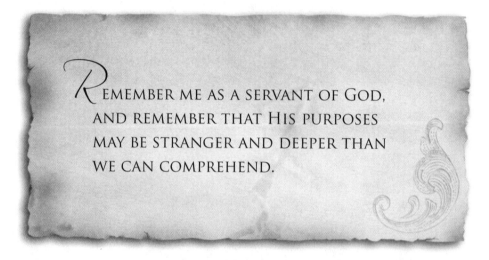

REMEMBER ME AS A SERVANT OF GOD, AND REMEMBER THAT HIS PURPOSES MAY BE STRANGER AND DEEPER THAN WE CAN COMPREHEND.

A caravan of people, donkeys, and carts does not move quickly. The first of the travelers began to move out of the inn yard, but it was nearly an hour before they were all on the road south. Leah rode on the back of the heavily laden donkey, while the three older children ran and played along the roadside. Miryam walked next to Yosef, holding his hand. She looked happy and hopeful in the clear autumn morning.

As for Yosef, he felt—what? A thousand things. Regret at leaving the only home he'd ever known. Fear at what lay ahead. But yes—anticipation, too. He'd spoken truly to Rahel—he and Miryam, the children and the unborn baby, were all in the hands of the Lord. Whatever happened from here on, they were following His will.

Chapter Fifteen

TRYING TO TRUST

A few days later, the journey to Bethle-hem seemed less like a good idea. Oh, Yosef still thought they were doing the right thing, and Miryam was sure of it, but such certainty was a thin thing against the reality of tiring days on the road, walking for long hours, seeking shelter by night, eating meals cooked hastily over an open fire by the roadside.

They had had to leave the caravan of travelers

they had first joined, for that group traveled more quickly than Yosef's family was able to do. The children simply could not keep up, walking, with a group of adults, nor could Miryam in her condition. As she grew more tired, she took turns with Yosef's little daughters, each of them taking a turn to ride on the donkey. And the donkey, laden with all their possessions plus at least one passenger, walked almost as slowly as Yehudah. The little boy tried hard to keep up with Yakov, who tried just as hard to keep up with Yosef, but they fell further behind till at last Yosef told the other travelers to go on without them.

For a day they traveled alone, but Yosef was wary, constantly scanning the road and the hillsides for bandits and outlaws. Roman soldiers were proud of their ability to keep the roads and countryside safe, but it was still not unusual to hear of attacks on travelers in open country. What could one man alone do to protect a woman and four children against an attacker? That night Yosef camped by the banks of the Jordan, and waited a full day till another family of travelers headed for the south came through. These travelers, also, were preparing to cross the Jordan to avoid going through Samaria, and their group included a father and grandfather along with a wife and children. Yosef and the other men agreed they could travel together at an easy pace and share the work and responsibility of the road.

So the days passed, making slow progress as the nights grew cooler and autumn deepened. In Jericho they stopped for three days because Shirah and Leah got coughs and were too sick to travel. Their fellow travelers were stopping there, at Jericho, and Yosef's family remained with them, waiting for his daughters to get better and another caravan to come along that they could travel with. He sat by the fireside in the courtyard of that home in Jericho, holding Shirah, looking across at Miryam with Leah in her arms. What if the girls didn't get well? What if they grew sicker and weaker, and one or both of them died here in Jericho? Had he been a complete fool to drag them on this long, hard journey?

But they grew well again, and another caravan passed, and once again they were on the road. They met many travelers these days, many of them hurrying back to their home towns in time to register for the census. As the nights grew colder, Yosef worried about how long it would take them to arrive in Bethlehem, and where they would stay there. Did his father still have kin in the town? He'd never heard him speak of any.

Miryam's progress grew slower every day, and one night she finally confessed that she was beginning to feel pains low in her abdomen. "Could they be birth-pains?" Yosef wondered aloud.

"Isn't it too soon?" Miryam asked, keeping her voice low so as not to disturb the children who slept nearby. "I don't expect the baby for another month, at least."

"Babies don't always keep to our schedules," Yosef told her. "Most of my four were born on time, but Yehudah was six weeks earlier than Leah expected him. She was working very hard, caring for Yakov, and thought that was perhaps why her pains started early. He was lucky to survive."

"So all this travel? This could bring the baby sooner?" Miryam sounded worried.

He reached for her hand in the darkness and held it in his. "It might," he said. "But you were determined God wanted this child born in Bethlehem. If He does, should He not protect the baby until we get there safely?"

"I hope He will." Her voice sounded weary, and close to tears. She squeezed his hand tightly. "I am trying so hard to trust Him, Yosef."

He was lying on his back, but he rolled over so they were lying face to face, close together in the dark. He reached up and felt the tears on her cheek. "You always seemed so sure of God's will in all this," he said. "I never guessed . . . I didn't know you felt any doubt."

"Not doubt, exactly. It's just . . . it seemed so real, all those months ago, when the angel came. And I know it *is* real, because the baby is here, inside me. But . . . sometimes it almost seems as if the Lord came, created this miracle, sent an angel to tell me the news, and then . . . left me to bear it all alone. I thought there would be . . . more."

"More angels? More miracles?"

SHE SQUEEZED HIS HAND TIGHTLY. "I AM TRYING SO HARD TO TRUST HIM, YOSEF.

"I don't know. Just . . . something more."

He put his arm around her as she wept softly in the dark, lying there on the cold, hard ground with only a thin blanket between her and the earth. He moved as close as her swollen belly would allow him, and touched her forehead lightly with his lips. "I'm sorry God hasn't sent you more angels, Miryam," he said finally. "But He hasn't left you to bear this alone, even if it feels that way. He sent me. Perhaps that was His other miracle."

She said nothing, but pressed her head into the hollow of his neck as if seeking shelter, and finally fell asleep.

The next day, at noon, they were within sight of Bethlehem.

Chapter Sixteen

NO ROOM AT THE INN

Once they were actually in Bethlehem— the children tired and restless, Miryam still having pains, even the donkey looking desperate for rest—Yosef wasn't sure where to go or what to do. In the busy village market-place he sought out the tax collector's booth and asked where he had to go to register for the census and pay his tax.

The small, balding man looked irritated. He

was already rolling up scrolls and putting away his tools as the afternoon's business drew to a close early on this Preparation day. "Come and see me tomorrow," he said. "No, tomorrow is Shabbat. Come see me on the first day of the week."

"Fine." He hadn't expected the business to be concluded instantly, after all. It would be a long process, no doubt.

Next he approached one of the elders sitting near the village gate. The older men, too, were getting ready to head to their homes, but one stopped to listen to Yosef's query.

"So your father was . . . who did you say? Yakov, son of Matthan?"

"Yakov bar Matthan bar Eleazar," Yosef said. "Yakov, my father, left Bethlehem to go to Galilee about 20 years ago, when I was a child. I think his father was already dead by then."

"Matthan? Oh yes, dead 25 years or more, easily." He turned to one of the other elders. "Wasn't he? Matthan son of Eleazar? When did he die?"

The other old man was hard of hearing and had to have the question repeated, but he agreed that Matthan had died before Caesar Augustus had become Emperor in Rome. "About the time the Romans made Herod king over us?" He spat on the dusty ground. "No, a few years after that—"

"So you remember Matthan bar Eleazar, then?" Yosef interrupted before the two men became too absorbed with reliving history.

"He had a son . . . married Asa's daughter and went off to the north."

"Yes! This is the grandson, here to register for the census," the first elder explained, gesturing toward Yosef. Several other old men gathered round to look at Yosef's family with mild interest. "Lot of people registering for that census," said one.

"Are there any of my father's kin left in Bethlehem?" Yosef asked.

The old men took some time discussing this, tracing genealogies and reminding each other who had married whose daughter, and who had died tragically young, before concluding that Yosef had no living cousins in Bethlehem. "The closest to you would be Caleb's family. You share the same great-grandfather, Eleazar," the man to whom he'd first spoken finally concluded. "But you can't call that close kin, can you?"

"No," Yosef agreed, wondering if it was worth his while to go look up the family of Caleb and make their distant relationship known. He tried a different approach. "My wife and children are weary, and we need a place to rest. Does anyone know of an inn where we can stay the night?"

"My wife takes travelers at our place, but every bed is full and we have two families on the floor in our courtyard," said the same man. "There's another inn. Not as good as ours, but they have a space for travelers to sleep and a place out in back to stable your beast." He quickly gave Yosef directions.

Yosef returned to Miryam and the children. Leah sagged in Miryam's arms, almost asleep, while the other three quarreled over a game they were playing with sticks in the dust, their voices tired and querulous.

"There's an inn at the other end of the village," he said, taking Leah from Miryam's arms. "Still a little bit of a walk. Why don't you ride on the donkey?" he suggested to his wife.

He passed Leah to Yakov and helped Miryam up onto the heavily laden donkey, trying to handle her gently. "I'm so tired," she murmured.

"The pains are still coming?"

She nodded.

Yosef rounded up the children and began to lead the donkey down the main road of the village. Perhaps when they got to the inn he could ask the woman of the house if there was a midwife nearby. He hoped it wasn't time yet for the baby to come, but

Miryam needed care and attention. He hoped that, given her condition, they could get a clean, private room inside the house—or even on the roof, though that would be cold—rather than having to bed down in the courtyard with others as they'd done so many nights on the road.

But when they finally reached the house that served as an inn, he could see that it was busy. People seemed to be everywhere, with their bags and bundles. Many were crowded around a fire in the middle of the courtyard, each family taking turns pushing closer to the coals to cook their own meals. Yosef left Miryam and the children in the road outside and made his way into the busy courtyard to find the man of the house.

"No room, sorry, none at all," the man said.

"Please. We can pay." Yosef thought of his small store of coins and wondered how long he could make them last. The journey here had left his purse lighter than he'd like. "My wife is with child, she needs to see a midwife. The babe could be born sooner than we thought—I must find a room for her."

"No rooms here at all," the man said. "Well, we've one room; the wife and I sleep there when there's no guests. But it's busy this week, very busy, and we have those Romans, you know?" He nodded at the soldiers. "Their officers are sleeping in the inside room, and the men on the floor of our main room. Everyone else is out in the courtyard—three families. Not so much as a spot to unroll a single bedroll—much less a big family like you've got there. And a baby on the way!" He nodded at Miryam.

"Where else can we go?" Yosef asked.

The man shrugged. "There's another inn, but I think they're busy too. Don't know what to tell you. You've no family in town you can stay with?"

"None that I know of. Is there anyone who might rent a room for a few coins?"

"You can ask around, I suppose."

"Could my wife and children stay here while I search for another place? Just to sit in the courtyard, please?"

The man frowned, then looked at Miryam and at the sleepy children. "All right, but only to sit and wait, not to sleep here. And mind you, it's almost sunset—soon be Shabbat. Nobody's going to want to do business then."

Yosef left Miryam, the children, the donkey and their bags in the corner of the crowded inn yard. He trudged up and down the nearest streets, knocking at every door. No one had a room they were willing to rent and at last, defeated and exhausted, with sunset coming on, he returned to the inn that had no room.

Miryam looked up hopefully at him. Perhaps, he amended, "desperate" might be a better word than "hopeful." She looked terrible, her hair tangled and sweaty, her face grimed from the road and tight with pain. He knew without asking that her pains were worse, and he tried to push back again the knowledge that this was happening, that the baby was coming in the midst of all this chaos and confusion, coming too early.

He had told Miryam about Yehudah's birth and told her the others were easy for Leah. Miryam would have known, living in the same village, that this was not true. She knew that Leah had died giving birth to her youngest child, her namesake who now lay sprawled in Miryam's arms, sleeping the sound sleep of an exhausted child.

Yosef had said nothing about Leah's death in childbed, because to do so would have worried Miryam and stirred up his own worst memories. But now, looking at the face of his young bride, he couldn't help remembering how Leah had looked that day when the pains started. She knew it was too early, knew she hadn't been feeling well, knew it was going to be a difficult delivery. He'd been banished to the courtyard when the midwife came, had sent the other children off to Rahel's but waited at home himself, pacing, listening to Leah's sharp, pain-filled cries.

He had gone into the house, finally, brushed past the midwife and the other women to kneel by her side and hold her hand through those last awful minutes. He'd been there, been able to say his goodbyes to her. It was the most painful memory of his life, and now he saw that same agony echoed in Miryam's face and eyes.

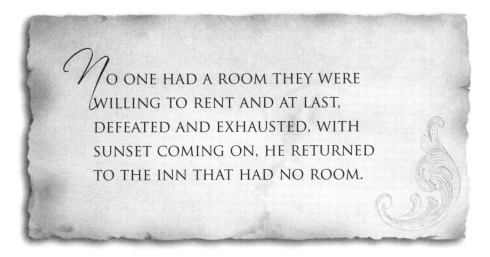

No one had a room they were willing to rent and at last, defeated and exhausted, with sunset coming on, he returned to the inn that had no room.

God of the Universe, would you make me suffer such a thing twice? You cannot be so cruel. You gave me Miryam and her child to care for—for You. Now protect them and bring me to a place where I can keep them safe.

He marched over to the owner of the inn once again. "I found no place to stay. I will pay any price you ask, but my wife's time is upon her and I need a bed to lay her in, a place with some privacy."

"Fine, fine then. Stay here if you can find a spot to unroll your blankets," the man said, waving his hand around the courtyard. "Pay me after Shabbat."

"Not here!" Yosef protested. "She can't give birth in a courtyard! Or in a room filled with Roman soldiers!"

Now, at last, he had the man's full attention. "She's going to have the baby now? Tonight, you think?"

"Yes! As soon as we have a place to lay our heads, I have to find a midwife."

"My sister's a midwife. I'll send someone for her. But I don't know where you can go—I can't turn Roman officers out of their room."

"Where, then? There must be some corner, some space—"

The man frowned. "Well . . . there's the place out back where the animals are stabled. Our own few beasts, and the soldiers' horses are there—just a shelter out of the wind, at the end of the pasture. You can go in there."

"Where you keep the animals?" Yosef echoed in disbelief. But then he shrugged. It would be private, anyway, which was what mattered most. "Send for the midwife," he said. "And lead us to your barn."

AT THAT MOMENT HE'D FINALLY REALIZED THAT HE LOVED HER AS UTTERLY AND ABSOLUTELY AS HE'D LOVED LEAH.

"Barn" was far too elegant a word for it. Behind the little inn stretched a long narrow field that ended in a rocky outcrop of hillside. Several horses and a cow grazed in the field, while at the end a crude shelter—a shallow cave with a wooden roof built out to provide a little more shelter—held food and water troughs for the animals.

"Plenty of clean hay here," the owner of the inn said, peering into the gloom with a flickering lamp he held aloft. Behind him trailed Yosef, holding Leah, Yakov leading the donkey with Miryam slumped over it, and Yehudah and Shirah trailing far behind, stumbling over the rutted field.

"Can you leave us the lamp?" Yosef asked.

"Fine, then, the lamp. You can build a little fire here to warm yourselves and cook your food if you're careful not to catch the grass on fire. I'll bring my sister out as soon as she gets here to see to your wife."

Yosef and Yakov piled up mounds of straw and spread out all their rolled blankets to make a bed for Miryam. Her face was pale and beaded with sweat as the pains squeezed her body. Yakov set Yehudah to work helping him build the fire as Yosef settled Leah down on another little pile of straw. She would probably have been warmer near Miryam, but this was no night to sleep beside her stepmother as she usually did, not if the baby came tonight. Shirah was hungry, so Yosef searched the packs for a little bread and cheese to give her and the boys. The children huddled around the tiny fire as he returned to Miryam and held her hand. She squeezed tight with each new wave of pain, and he spoke to her in a low soothing voice.

It came to him, now that he had time to think of it, that at that moment in the courtyard when he saw the pain she was in, when she reminded him of Leah in those last awful hours, he'd finally realized that he loved her as utterly and absolutely as he'd loved Leah. A different love, yes, for a very different woman, but it seemed a man could fall in love twice, and here he was once again holding the hand of a woman he loved, terrified of losing her.

Nothing else matters, he told himself. Whoever her baby was, whoever his father was— God himself or some other man—it didn't matter. Whether they ever went back to Nazareth or stayed here in Bethlehem or traveled even farther, it didn't matter. All that mattered was that Miryam and her child should live through this night, and that he, Yosef, get to fulfill his promise to God to care for Miryam and raise her child as his own. *Yes, Lord, yes,* he vowed. *I will never leave her or forsake her. Only bring her and the baby safely through this hour.*

The evening wore on, through minutes that seemed like hours and hours that seemed like years. He wondered what had become of the promised midwife, but he didn't want to get up and leave Miryam to go looking. The children settled down to sleep on the other side of the little shelter, the boys on either side forming a protective wall around their little sisters. He covered them with all the cloaks he could find, since Miryam had all the blankets, kissed them and told them not to worry. Shirah was troubled by Miryam's cries of pain, but Yosef assured her it was all part of having a baby, and that by morning they might have a new little brother.

When the children were settled he went back to Miryam's side, holding her hand again. A couple of horses wandered over to drink from the trough. Their heavy, hot breath and sweaty flanks gave off more warmth than the smoldering fire did.

It seemed an eternity of Miryam's cries and pains before he saw three people walking toward them over the field, carrying another lamp. Three women—the midwife, her sister-in-law who operated the inn, and the innkeeper's daughter.

"Now, what have we here?" the midwife asked as she bent to examine Miryam. "How often are the pains coming, my dear? How many breaths can you get between them? Have you counted? No? Let's count, now, then. Kezia, bring me that water."

With the women surrounding Miryam, Yosef was quickly pushed off to the side, just as he had been when Leah had her babies. He went to stir up the fire a little, finding some more sticks of wood to add to it, then checked on the children. The younger ones slept soundly, but Yakov's dark eyes blinked open and met his.

"Not asleep?"

"I can't."

"It's all right. Everything will be all right," he assured the boy. "Do you want to come for a little walk with me?"

"Yes, please," he said, sitting up and slipping his feet back into his sandals. He put his hand in his father's—a childish gesture Yakov seldom allowed himself anymore—and they walked across the field, away from the busy women and Miryam's cries.

"Why does it have to hurt so much?" Yakov asked.

"For the same reason it hurts for a man to push a plough or swing a hammer. It's the good honest hurt of hard labor, and the Scriptures say it was God's curse to man and woman when they sinned. But even His curses are gifts, my son. You'll see in the morning, when Miryam has a fine strong baby boy."

"You know it'll be a boy? When Mama had her babies you told us there was no way to be sure."

"No." Yosef hesitated, not sure how much to say to this boy who was so nearly a man. "But Miryam's baby is—different. Special. Miryam and I each had a vision about him before he was born, and in my vision I was told that he would be a boy, named Yeshua, and that God would have a special work for him to do."

"Really? Like Isaac, or Samuel, or Samson?" Yakov said. How quick the boy's mind was! He was a fine little carpenter, but Yosef hoped he could offer him more education, too—a chance to read the Scriptures for himself. Miryam's baby was indeed going to be special, but all his children were precious to him, and surely the Lord had a plan for each of them.

"Yes, like those children of old," Yosef said.

"So—if you had a vision, then Miryam won't die having this baby, will she?" Yakov's voice trembled just a little.

"I . . . don't think so," Yosef said. All day he had been trying to push from his mind the fact that neither his own vision nor Miryam's had promised that she would live to raise the child, only that the child would be born and grow to a great destiny. *Lord, don't tear the woman I love from me a second time! Don't leave me alone again!* As if in answer another of Miryam's shrieks rose into the night sky. Yakov shivered, and Yosef wrapped his cloak around the boy's shoulders.

"You're thinking of your mother," he said. "So am I. I loved her very much, Yakov, but God knows best."

"I don't—I don't love Miryam like Mama," Yakov confessed. "But she's kind, and pretty, and it's good for the little ones to have a mother. And for you to have a wife, I think," he said, sounding like a little old man. "I don't want her to die."

"I don't think she will, son," Yosef said. "She will live, and have many children, and help raise you and your brother and sisters. And you must continue being a good big brother—especially to this special baby, the one who will be born tonight."

"I will. I'll look after him," Yakov promised solemnly.

Yosef looked up at the sky. It was still dark, and he could not tell what watch of the night it was. The moon had risen, washing the field and the houses with silver light. He turned back toward the stable and the fire and the women.

One of the women—not the midwife, the younger one—came out to meet them. "No baby yet, but soon. She's begun to push."

"Then let us hope it won't be long," Yosef said. "Go back to the others, Yakov, and keep them warm. Try to get a little sleep yourself." He went back with the girl to see Miryam. The women hovered protectively over her, her body arched with pain and effort as she let out another rending cry.

He squatted near the fire, poking at the coals, murmuring prayers under his breath. Miryam's cries and the midwife's words of encouragement were like a ritual chant that went on and on, the tempo rising as the moment drew nearer.

"You there! What's your name? Come see your son!"

"What?" Yosef's feet moved even before his mind had grasped the words. He knelt at Miryam's side as the midwife cut the cord with her knife and washed the squalling, bloody bundle.

At first Yosef barely saw the baby. He bent down to touch Miryam's face, to put his lips against her forehead. "Are you well?" he asked. "It's done, my love. You've done it. Good work."

"Is he—the baby? Is he—alive? Well?"

"Yes, yes, my love. The midwife is getting him ready now. Here, here he is." Yosef took the tightly wrapped baby from the midwife. The coarse homespun cloth in which the baby was wrapped looked almost brilliantly clean in the muddy, dirty stable. Yosef looked at the red little face, the only thing showing among the swaddling. The baby's eyes were screwed shut, then suddenly opened to look straight into his, surprisingly dark and keen.

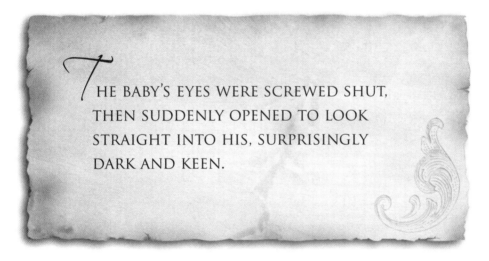

THE BABY'S EYES WERE SCREWED SHUT, THEN SUDDENLY OPENED TO LOOK STRAIGHT INTO HIS, SURPRISINGLY DARK AND KEEN.

"You haven't even asked if it's a boy!" the midwife laughed.

"It is, though, isn't it?" Yosef said, handing the baby to Miryam as she bared her breast and one of the women guided the baby's mouth toward it. "A boy? And his name is Yeshua."

"Yeshua." The woman nodded. "A good name."

The other woman, the innkeeper's wife, looked up. "What's this? Who's coming now?"

Another group of people traipsed across the field, this time led by the owner of the inn. These were men, several of them, with rough loud voices.

"You'll never believe this!" the innkeeper called. "Has she had her baby yet?"

"Just now," Yosef said, getting to his feet as if to forestall these men and keep them away from his wife and new baby.

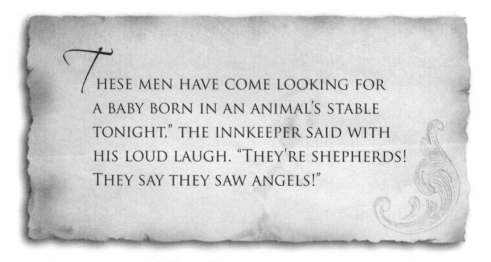

THESE MEN HAVE COME LOOKING FOR A BABY BORN IN AN ANIMAL'S STABLE TONIGHT," THE INNKEEPER SAID WITH HIS LOUD LAUGH. "THEY'RE SHEPHERDS! THEY SAY THEY SAW ANGELS!"

"Good, because these men have come in from the hills looking for a baby born in an animal's stable tonight," the innkeeper said with his loud laugh. "They're shepherds! They say they saw angels!"

"What?" Yosef turned at once to the nearest of the men, a rough swarthy fellow in a heavy cloak. "You saw angels?"

"They're mad!" the innkeeper laughed. "Been passing a flask of wine around all night, most likely." But Yosef was no longer paying attention.

"I swear to you, sir," the shepherd said, laying a hand on his heart. "We're not drunk and not mad. We were out on the hills with the sheep, and suddenly there was a bright light, and an angel told us that Israel's Deliverer was born tonight in Bethlehem, laid in an animal's feeding trough."

"Then there were angels everywhere!" another man broke in. "They started to sing. 'Glory to God,' they sang, and 'peace on earth.'"

"They did!" the first man insisted. "We all saw it, not just one of us. We all saw it, and we decided to come here and find the baby, to see if it was true."

"It is true," Yosef said, ignoring the stares of the innkeeper and the women. "My wife and I—each of us had a vision, months ago. I saw an angel too, and he told me that this child would save His people."

The youngest of the shepherds, a boy about Yakov's age, pushed forward. "Can we see him?"

The midwife bustled forward. "Now, you can't come and bother a woman with a new baby. Go away, all of you." She made a little shooing motion with her hands, as if chasing chickens from the yard.

"No, wait." Yosef looked at Miryam over the woman's head, and met her eyes. What he read there told him all he needed to know. She slipped the baby from her breast, covered herself up and tried to sit up. She lifted the baby, who was sleeping now, and Yosef bent to take him.

The men shuffled closer, till they were almost inside the shelter. Yosef held little Yeshua, who slept soundly as the men peered at him, and when Yosef settled onto the ground beside Miryam, the men knelt on the ground as if kneeling before a king.

Miryam squeezed Yosef's hand and said something. Yosef bent down to hear her soft words.

"More angels," she whispered. "He sent more angels, after all."

The sky was turning from black to grey. Dawn came at last as again and again the men from the fields told about their vision, their words stumbling over each other as Miryam and Yosef, too, told about the angels they had seen.

As they sat there talking while the baby slept, the other children awakened and moved closer, eager for a glimpse of their new brother. The innkeeper and his wife shuffled away, but Yosef barely noticed. He took Miryam's hand in his. She grew quiet, and her breathing became steady and even. She had fallen asleep. Yosef put the baby back into her arms, close to her body, and Yeshua slept on.

He looked up to see that more people had gathered—the other travelers from the inn, edging closer, wanting to hear about the angels and see the baby.

"Is it really?" one man asked Yosef as he looked at Yeshua asleep in Miryam's arms. "Did you really have a vision saying this child would deliver us?"

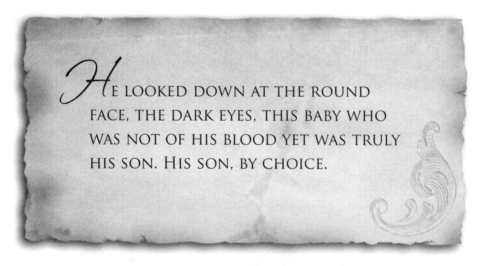

HE LOOKED DOWN AT THE ROUND FACE, THE DARK EYES, THIS BABY WHO WAS NOT OF HIS BLOOD YET WAS TRULY HIS SON. HIS SON, BY CHOICE.

"Who can believe it?" a woman said. "Angels appearing to shepherds and Galileans! A Messiah from Galilee?"

"It's very strange," another voice said.

Someone had stirred up the fire again, and some of the travelers had brought food. While Miryam and Yeshua slept on, everyone gathered around the fire to share a bowl of barley and some bread and dried fish and dates. One of the shepherds had a small clay pipe and began to play music softly as the innkeeper crossed the field again with a pitcher and some cups. "Wine for everyone!" he announced as the sun slipped over the horizon. He poured a cup and lifted it. "Just in case—who knows, we might have a Messiah born here this morning!"

Everyone took a cup and raised it in salute. Yosef smiled at the shepherds—they were, after all, the only ones other than himself and Miryam who really understood. Everyone else had come out of curiosity, to celebrate the birth of a baby, which was always a happy event. Nobody else really believed in the angels and visions, but he knew.

The sleeping baby in Miryam's arms began to stir and whimper, and Yosef took him and cradled him, rocking him gently. "Ooh, let me hold him," one of the women offered, but Yosef shook his head. "No, I'll keep him for now."

He looked down at the round face, the dark eyes, this baby who was not of his blood yet was truly his son. His son, by choice.

More angels. Maybe the third visit was the final proof he'd needed. For in this moment, holding Yeshua in his arms, Yosef finally, for the first time in months, felt utterly free from doubt. He had stepped out in faith, but now his faith had turned to certainty. For the moment not only doubt but also fear and worry were pushed aside. There was room in his heart for nothing but the most amazing love.

Messiah for the Twenty-first Century

JESUS said, I AM He Who walked among the Ancients, your fathers since Adam,
     I AM Messiah come to Earth, Gone back to Heaven, Soon to return for you,
I AM the Vine intertwining through your life,

I walk with you through dirty dishes, bills, and laundry stacked to the ceiling,
     I walk with you through flying arrows from your enemies,
Through happiness, through children's laughter, through silence from the ones you love
     Who never call or write,
     Through illness, joys . . .

People try to second guess how things will go, according to their traditions,
And act surprised at My miracles that get you through your days—
I CAN do them, you know—or not.
     Depend on Me either way—I AM on the move, I see what's coming,
     You can trust My next move.

In the ordinary hum of passing Time, I may close a door—
     (Did you hear it almost slam shut?)
Pay attention.
     Another door is opening—
     An Anything but Ordinary Door.

—Rhoda Wills